ISBN:1536902578
2016 Els Boot Rotterdam Netherlands

No part of this publication may be reproduced, distributed, or transmitted in any form or by any means, including photocopying, recording, or other electronic or mechanical methods, without the prior written permission of the publisher, except in the case of brief quotations embodied in critical reviews and certain other non commercial uses permitted by copyright law.

Skopelos

A narrative about a quest for Ithaca

Els Boot

"Sing to me of the man, Muse, the man of twists and turns driven time and again off course, once he had plundered the hallowed heights of Troy..."

Homerus

I

I get up. There's no alarm, I'm awake before it goes off at all times. I look through the glass façade in my bedroom, out across the Betuwe landscape. It is a nice day today. Getting up is not difficult; every day is like a new adventure for me.
Or so I thought. Until I found out that I do not like adventures. They feel like a violation of my normal ways. I feel inconvenienced, uncomfortable, lost even.
I know that now. But you don't. I'm writing this story afterwards so I already know the end of my story.
I have chosen to do so because I hope it will give you a peek inside my world, so you can follow me in my reasoning and considerations, and you can understand me because that's what I've been needing a lot recently, to simply be understood.
It's my life story, a travel log if you want to put it that way. My personal travel log. I am proud, because the journey that I'm going to tell you about is the hardest thing I ever experienced. I am a man of few words, find it very hard to talk about my feelings. You might

consider my language use quite business-like, but believe me when I tell you that I know how it feels now to experience emotions for the first time in my life, and this makes me happy indeed. I am old and don't have many years left. But the ones I still have will be the most beautiful, I know that now. I got to know myself.

Anyway, I decide to get up. Put my feet in my slippers, which are waiting for me neatly next to my bed, every single day. My robe is hanging on the closet door. Then the alarm goes off.
It's seven o'clock. When I walk down the open staircase I feel very satisfied with this particular choice again, like every day. It has a beautiful black iron frame and the stairs are made from gorgeous cherry wood. I look around briefly downstairs. This is also a habit that I repeat daily. My life is full of rituals, I do not know why. My living room is on one side and the dining room on the other, there's a cooking island in between both rooms. I'm still very satisfied with the transformation of my 18th century farmhouse. I bought it twenty-eight years ago and had it radically renovated and restored eighteen years ago.

I thought about everything, which took me a lot of time. First there were endless discussions with the architect. I had a clear picture of how it all should be, but had to leave the direction to the architect. It was extremely hard for me to let go of my ideas, to trust him, to allow changes. It left me feeling stressed and tired. It has always been hard for me to depend on others, that is just my nature.

Then came the endless search for the right tiles, good colour combinations, the interior of the bathroom, the layout of the closet. You name it. I have studied stacks of brochures, infinitely searching for the right colour for the wooden floors, the art on the walls, the sculptures you can now find in the corners of various rooms. My God, no one had told me it would be such a nuisance.

My friends say it's because I'm a perfectionist. I think they are right, but now, even after all that work, I still enjoy the fruits of my hard labour and thus the effort and money for the restoration were well spent in my opinion. Every day of my life, I feel comfortable and at home in the midst of my own creation. Everything is in order.

I cleaned up the coffee cup and wine glass I used last night. I always do this just before bedtime; I like it when everything is clean and quiet when I come downstairs in the mornings. I even fluff the pillows on the couch a bit before I go to bed, and smooth the cover of the couch. It makes it look as if it is brand new, which gives me a sense of satisfaction.

The gravel is crackling under my feet. I pick up the newspaper from the mailbox and go back inside. Every day I hope the delivery man hasn't forgotten me, while I walk those five meters, there is no newspaper in the mailbox today. This disturbs my morning ritual and brings me down.
I'm not a nit-picker, even though I might sound that way. It's just my morning ritual. I found out that everyone has a morning ritual. But because I have never shared my home and life with someone else, it took me some time to realise this.

But let me introduce myself. My name is Paul van den Berg. I am sixty years old, unmarried and work as an asset manager for a large financial institution. It's what I've been doing during most of my working life.

I grew up here, in the Betuwe region, in a warm and loving but also very strict Calvinist family. I have two sisters and three brothers; I'm the oldest of them all. We went to church twice every Sunday. I wore a black suit with a shirt and tie, even when I was very young. It was one of the regulations of our church. The Lord God was to be honoured with respect and neat clothing was a part of that. We were not allowed to play outside after church and I remember those idle Sundays as pure torture. Especially in summer, when the sun was shining and I could think of so many things which would be more fun than listening to my father reading from the Bible. I was ashamed of these thoughts and was convinced that the Lord God would punish me for them sooner or later.

My parents were loving and good parents. They were dedicated to all of us. Only on Sundays did they change their ways, my father's voice even changed when he read from the Bible. He read in a soft singsong voice, perched on a straight kitchen chair and expecting us to sit up straight. We were not allowed to wiggle or whisper during the Scripture readings, and we could only drink from our tea cups and take nibbles of our biscuits once he nodded almost invisibly and thus gave his permission. My mother made sure we obliged him and fumbled with our clothes and ties occasionally, when she thought something was not straight or creased because of our playful childlike attitudes on those hard chairs.

My mother was a housewife and took care of daily business. My father considered the house and household to be her domain and never interfered with her choices for things like the interior, the food or the clothing for the children. He showed due respect for my mother this way. Sometimes I think that it was his way of trying to make amends with all the restrictions that our faith imposed on my mother. Perhaps he felt guilty towards her; after all, my mother was an intelligent woman with many talents. Yet I firmly believe that my mother had a comfortable and free life despite those limitations.

Yes, my mother was an intelligent woman. She graduated from grammar school. When all the work in and around the house was finally finished, she read. I saw that once when I was sick. She sat down that day in the comfortable chair that belonged to my father and read. She read everything my father had gathered in his study and could spend hours in major bookstores in the city. My mother was a well-read woman.

Very occasionally, she joined in intellectual conversations my father had with members of the church or with colleagues. I observed this. Her contribution was sincerely appreciated and even my father gleamed with pride. I believe he genuinely loved her very much.

Sometimes, my mother did a few translation jobs for the church. She fluently spoke four languages and read Latin and Ancient Greek with ease. While I was still in grammar school, she helped me with those subjects. She was a very lively and cheerful woman. Balanced and always willing to help others with their various problems. She was firm and buxom, with thick blond hair that she put up on her head. Her face was a healthy bright pink. Her eyes were dark and deep. When she moved, her clothes flowed with her; it was as if she was always dancing. It made me happy to look at my mother because everything from her emanated with cheerfulness, her dancing pace, her hair, her loud voice. When she was busy, and she almost always was, she spoke to everyone around her without actually saying a word. She gave everyone the feeling of being important. I never felt overlooked in her presence. Everyone loved her I think.

After school we laughed a lot while drinking tea. It was my mother who taught me, that sometimes you were allowed to deviate from the austerity which the Bible prescribed.
Once when we got home from school, she baked cookies, a lot of them. We were all given one cookie each. We ate it slowly and chewed deliberately on every bite, enjoying it should last as long as possible. My mother was clearly enjoying it too, as she closed her eyes and made approving noises while chewing. When we finished the cookie she looked at us and said: "We'll have another one", and offered us a second biscuit. That one was finished a lot faster and before we knew it, my mother had emptied the contents of the cookie jar on the table and we all grabbed at the cookies cheerfully. My mother ate eagerly and cookie crumbs stuck to her pink cheeks. We laughed, she laughed. When all the cookies were finished she looked at us.
"Now we need to ask our Lord for forgiveness for our gluttony and thank him for these delicious cookies," she said almost seriously. And so we did.

I loved my mother. When she died, I lived through a kind of depression during a long period. She had always been my inner compass and anchor point.

My father was a professor at the Free University in Amsterdam, where he taught Dutch law. He specialized in corporate law and had a consultancy bureau on the side, which he used to perform consultancy projects from time to time for a select few. Besides his work, he did many things as a volunteer. I remember that he was often gone in the evenings, or working in his study for some association or foundation. My mother used to bring him his tea upstairs. But when we went to bed, he came out of his room and read to us sitting on the edge of the bed. He was very good at it; he created voices for each character and let his face tell a part of the story. When he was finished, he tucked us in and kissed us gently on our foreheads.

My father was not a cheerful person, not like my mother. He rarely smiled, and I don't think I've ever seen him laughing out loud. His facial expression was predominantly gloomy. That didn't mean he was a grumpy man though, or that he was easily irritated or angry. He was actually gentle and rarely punished us.

If punishment was necessary, he left this to my mother who was a lot tougher. He was a hard worker who never complained and seemed very pleased with his work and family. On Saturdays, he incessantly tried to help my mother with small chores around the house. My mother let him but the result was almost always dramatic. He was not a craftsman and was certainly not skilful. On Sundays, my father changed as I already wrote. He walked through the house in a black suit, slightly bent. The black of his suit made the colour of his face look even pale in comparison. I almost felt sorry for him, because it was so obvious that something was weighing heavy upon him.
I actually never knew my father: I must honestly say I never knew who he truly was. This made his death even sadder, shortly after my mother passed away. It was as if his despondent existence became even more despondent and pointless, after the death of the woman he cherished so.

We were a total of six children. I have three brothers and two sisters. I am the oldest; my sister Marian came after me, then my three brothers and then the youngest, my sister Esther. We played a lot with each other and unlike what I experienced in other families, we rarely fought among us boys.

I barely kept in touch with two of my brothers. Our lives have grown apart from each other. They both joined an even stricter Calvinistic church than the one we grew up with. I still see my youngest brother on birthdays. He's like my father, drags his feet behind his wife and children to all mandatory birthdays, caring and gentle as he is. My oldest sister Marian visits me regularly. While she loathes my life, partly due to religious considerations, I am still her older brother. If there's something she worries about, I am the first she runs to. I see my youngest sister Esther the most. But not on birthdays; she doesn't show herself at those since the death of our parents. I can't blame her. When she was twenty she left God and the Church to live with a Turkish Muslim. She still does and they have two children. Despite the shame she brought into our family, my parents welcomed her Turkish friend with open arms and did so with an almost divinely dictated act of kindness. My parents were good people.

The adventure

I am sitting at my kitchen island, drinking my Nespresso coffee and reading the newspaper. Once I finish my coffee I go back upstairs. I take a shower and cherish the smell of a new shower gel I bought at the perfumery last week. It smells divine. I shave and put on some expensive facial cream that I received from a friend, it feels very nice and cool on my skin. I am in doubt about my perfume though. Should I even wear a scent today? I decide not to. I check my eyebrows and clean my ears. I'm done quickly with my hair: I don't have much left on my head.
Last night I already laid out the suit I'm wearing today, it is hanging in my walk-in closet. I always do this the evening before because I'm afraid to hurry in the morning and then, in my rush, choose a mismatch. I observe my collection of beautifully tailored suits and shirts with great pleasure. My ties, of which I have as many as two hundred, are hung neatly next to each other. But I only use one hanger per tie,

otherwise I have to dig for a tie which I very much dislike.

I put on a light blue-grey suit that I have had made in New York five years ago. It is made of a soft, supple fabric. It looks a little bit too youthful on me, but apparently that was exactly my intention when I picked it yesterday evening. I'm wearing a soft pink shirt underneath, and a somewhat brighter red-pink tie. I look in the mirror and wonder what came over me last night when I picked out this combination, but I don't doubt; I never doubt my choices.

Since the weather is nice and I'm wearing a light suit, I chose light-grey suede shoes yesterday. They feel comfortable and are exceptionally elegant in my opinion. I don't know what other people will think.

When I'm back in the kitchen, I eat a sandwich I prepared yesterday and is therefore waiting for me in the fridge. I then press a lemon, pour the juice into a glass and add half a cup of water, otherwise it is so acidic. I have been doing that for years. Someone once told me, that consuming a lemon with each breakfast is a healthy habit.

I leave my house at eight o'clock sharp. One of my privileges at our company is that I don't have to take traffic jams into account. They'll simply see me when I get there. My secretary knows this, plus my first appointments are never before nine. It's nice and peaceful to have this routine. I walk to the garage and still consider it a pity that I could not realize an indoor entry during the restoration of the farmhouse. The municipality would not allow it since the farm is a monument. That's just the way it is. Luckily, I don't have to open the garage door myself every day: I have a neatly functioning electrical system. The door buzzes open and I can see my two cars.

A silver Corvette that I never drive, in fact I don't even know how I let someone talk me into buying the thing. I have absolutely no affinity with cars. My other car is a Mercedes CLS coupé. Way too expensive and way too large for an old man like me. But I had to purchase something with style, a friend of mine told me. "You cannot drive a Beetle to work when you hold such an important position."

Some people in senior positions are able to pull it off though. When I see Steve Jobs on TV, in shirtsleeves, baggy pants and no tie I definitely think of him as brave. But he's a hippie. I have to bear in mind the reservations that people might have towards me and so I feel I must look impeccable. A friend told me that this way of thinking is nonsense, that we just create our own straitjackets that way. He's right, I think.

It is quiet on the road today. I always listen to Radio 1, along with reading the daily newspaper, so that I am well informed. When I'm at work on time I read the Financial Times, which is a must considering my position. I really like my habits, they provide me with peace and structure.

Only eight days of work left, by then it's time for my annual holiday. I am not especially looking forward to it, since I haven't got a clue about what to do or where to go. Liesbeth, my secretary, is constantly asking me about my plans so she can book me a ticket. For weeks I have been finding folders on my desk of great holiday destinations. That is nosy, but nice of her. Because she always picks fun destinations: she knows me well. Package holidays to big cities with lots of cultural activities, as well as the opportunity to look for special antique pieces of furniture. A hobby of mine.

I'll continue with my story.
So I grew up in a balanced and harmonious family. And although I have never seen my father kissing or

caressing my mother, everyone in our family knew that there was a deep love between those two people. Yet I can remember that, when I was around thirteen years old, I no longer felt at ease. I feared the wrath of God for all the sinful things I had done and thought about. I was in puberty, but according to my mother I still behaved exemplary. The truth was that I wanted to escape the divine punishment that seemed more and more inevitable by behaving well. But inevitable it was!

I fell in love for the first time in the second year of grammar school. I thought about sex, but that was my least sinful deed I think. Because the most confusing and frightening one was that I had fallen in love with a boy! His name was Hans, and he was physically more developed for his age than most of the boys in my class. He was tall and slender, had broad shoulders, narrow hips and clearly pronounced biceps. He was not reformed but evangelical, I heard my parents whispering during an introduction evening for parents and students. Their eyes barely concealed their disapproval. And that was apparently also the reason he was dressed differently, and wore his long blond hair on his forehead like a Beatle. My unconditional love and passion for Hans ruined my grammar school years. During the days I didn't know how to behave, stayed as far away from Hans as possible, and in bed at night I lay writhing in misery because of all the feelings that were playing tricks on me. I still learned how to get along with the boys during that period, doing things boys do and talking like one of the guys.

A few years ago I searched for Hans on the Internet. I found him on LinkedIn. He is married, has two children and has a career in the educational sector. Later that evening, I figured that he could see that I had viewed his profile. It actually kept me awake all night. What must he have thought of me?

But what felt like the biggest and most difficult hurdle was the way my father interrogated me regularly about girls, when I was in my graduating class. I would go to college, that was for certain, and he obviously wanted me to become engaged to a girl from our church before I would leave. Once, during such a conversation, I caught my mother's glance while she was observing me from her usual spot in the room. Her eyes, her face... My mother definitely knew back then. Still, I never talked to her about my homosexuality, and she in turn never tried to discuss it with me. Even being the joyful and loving mother that she was; this would be a bridge too far for her, I think.

In our village and our church, it would be considered a shame to our family if I would openly come out for my homosexuality. Next to that, I was convinced that my feelings would eventually change if I just lived a proper life and prayed a lot. Perhaps then I would even be allowed to enter the Kingdom of God. Because I had learned that homosexuality was an illness. A disease that could be cured. I didn't want to disappoint my parents. They were good and sweet, and so I pretended to be interested in girls. I started dating girls once I reached the appropriate age, girls from our church even. The biggest advantage was that any form of physical contact was strictly forbidden before marriage in our religious circles. The girls with whom I went out, who secretly wanted to fool around, took me for a religious fanatic. I left it that way, since it was actually convenient.

I was the oldest, the figurehead of the fruit which God had entrusted to my parents. And that came with certain obligations.

Luckily I was able to escape eventually. I graduated brilliantly for my final exams and became enrolled as a first year student of Economics at the Erasmus University in Rotterdam. The daily commute to Rotterdam proved to be too much however, and so my father arranged a room with a 'brother' in Rotterdam.

For some reason, I finally picked up the courage to get out of there during my third year. I had become friends with a classmate. His name was Ronald and he lived in a three room flat that his parents had bought for him. He had a room available and asked me to move in. I knew he wasn't gay, so his request confused me at first. But I liked his cheerfulness, his student-wantonness and his wit and intelligence. I was curious about the real student life that, while I lived in the house of the friend of my father, had passed me by completely. So I agreed.

That sense of freedom and joy, the eating out of boxes, the parties and the music: it was all new to me and I experienced many hilarious evenings with him. It was there that I drank my first beer, and became drunk for the first time. My parents have never visited me there.

My friends think of my religious background as bleak. I do not agree with them. As I already wrote, our family was a cheerful family, albeit within the limits of what the Lord and church permitted us, but still, I never experienced my childhood as bleak. There was only a sense of inhibition because of my insecurity about my sexual orientation, I suppose.

I went home every weekend. Of course I stalled it to the extreme, because I did not feel like going to church and reading the Bible. But I did go. Visited the church twice every Sunday and listened to my father as he read from the Bible, his voice becoming a soft lilting sound that didn't suit him but nonetheless indicated that he felt deeply touched by what he was reading.
My youngest sister was always happy when I returned again. She secretly asked me in the hallway how it was in Rotterdam, with all the parties and no parents around.
She has been the only one who brought up my homosexuality years ago, once when she was visiting

me. I could not talk to her about it, although I'm still immensely grateful for that failed conversation with her. When I think back tears well up in my eyes. She eventually left God and the church as I wrote earlier.

I've been thinking a lot about my inhibitions. Some of my friends blame society, since homosexuality still hasn't been totally accepted. According to them, it is our environment that makes young gay men feel lonely and abandoned as they begin to uncover their sexuality. I believe this way of thinking is a bit too easy, for how does it explain that there are gay people, including my friends, who are more than able to enter into normal relationships? Who don't feel as embarrassed as I do when dealing with women? I think it's my personality that makes it impossible for me to be able to provoke. I am quite similar to my father, I believe.

I drive into the parking garage of the company where I work. I have my own private spot, a privilege gained after many years of dutiful service. Or rather; after structurally bringing in high profits for our company during many years. It does not bother me though. I'm business-like and expect appropriate remuneration for my efforts.

The approaching holiday is still stuck in my head. Eight days. But I still don't know what to do. Since I can remember I have been visiting all the big cities. I feast on the culture, good food and exciting encounters with the friends I made in recent years. This entails parties of a certain allure with sultry nights. It's the kind of sexual experience that normal people might remember from their childhoods: a little sneaky, a tad unhinged.

I can only write about it now, after all those years. The duality of my existence. You don't know why because you don't know the end of the story yet. But I do.

I will try to explain why so many gay people indulge in these sorts of orgy-like one-night stands.

I have a lot of friends, most of them are gay. My heterosexual friends are all couples; I find it difficult to be friends with women only. I have a bond with some friends, you could say almost a real relationship, but without the sex. I discuss my soul stirrings with them, I also buy my furniture and clothes with them. I eat with them, or we visit the theatre. Almost all of them are older men like me. Almost all of them are alone. Only a few of them are in a solid relationship and do or do not live together. The friends with whom I occasionally share my bed are all much younger than me. On my bad and guilty moments I sometimes think I use them as my hookers, but that thought is way too dark. They are my friends and I feel responsible for them, I just don't take them to the theatre or the library.

Sex between two men is sinful, or so I have been taught since childhood. And even though I'm intelligent enough to distance myself from this nonsense, apparently this belief still stirs deep within me. That sex is forbidden and sinful. So it all plays out in relative anonymity and with a sneaky touch. I keep these relationships far away from my 'real' relationships, real meaning fitting into the heterosexual world in which we live. I envy the gay men who have managed to shake off this psychological split personality and are able to live as full human beings. I am unable to do that. My personality has me trapped in a conception of decency and about what belongs and what does not, a conception that makes me unable to live a normal life.

Sometimes I go looking for antiques during my vacations to France or Italy. That's my favourite pastime. And I should tell you that I managed to create quite a beautiful collection over the years. I have many friends in France and Italy who, like me, share that passion. During recent years I noticed that I prefer to go on antiques holidays, rather than another trip to New York, Paris or London. My relationships with my antique friends are clearly more than just good sex. After all, I too am in need of commonality.

While I'm in the elevator on the way to my office, I wonder whether I should go to France or Italy again. I will have to come up with an answer for my secretary soon; she is becoming nervous.

I get off on the fifth floor and walk down the corridor. I have forbidden my secretary to run up directly behind me with a thousand questions and endless stacks of paper. I explained to her that I appreciate being able to take off my jacket calmly first. The truth is that I briefly want to breathe in the atmosphere of my office, with the door closed. I know she is waiting behind the door of her office when she hears me. She waits until I'm inside. Then she counts to ten. At least I think so. I've tried doing it myself and seriously, after exactly ten seconds she sticks her head around the door of my office.

Today, she is already waiting for me in the hallway when I walk out of the elevator and scurries behind me to my room. To be a step ahead of my obvious displeasure about it, she exclaims; "You look nice today, Paul. That tie… I've never seen it before!"

I look at her. I cannot be mad at her, she's so dedicated. I love her.

"Liesbeth, I've had that tie for three years," I tell her. She puts a pile of papers on my desk.

"This is for today," she says. I keep waiting in the middle of my office. This is not everything. She would never ignore my instructions for these documents alone. There must be something important, something she is going to tell me now.

"There was a call for you from Greece. A nice man." She looks at me in a significant way, but I don't respond to her intimate glance. I am unable to do so.

"What is so special about it that made you decide to ambush me immediately?"

She responds enthusiastically; "You have never been called from Greece. Besides, do they even have assets to manage over there?"

"I don't know anyone in Greece and maybe they have become wise."

"Anyway, it's a private call," she tells me, "shall I call them back for you immediately?"

I hear a friendly male voice on the other end of the line. He speaks perfect English. He's a notary and calling from an island I've never heard of: Skopelos. He kindly explains to me that he is handling a will, and that will is the reason he called.

"Luckily, you were not hard to find Mr. van den Berg. On the twenty-ninth of April, your friend Dimitris Kroprantzelas passed away. My sincerest condolences. We are very shocked by his death here on Skopelos; he was a familiar face and an appreciated person in our relatively small community. I imagine that you were also shocked when you heard the news. You probably already knew through others. The testament has been opened last week and you are referred to therein."

I'm afraid to say anything, I'm not that good with primary reactions, but I do not know anyone named that way... Before I allow a vague image of a distant past to appear in my mind, I ask the man if he is certain that I am the correct person. He is sure. He has my home address, which was mentioned in the will, and has my birthdate. He already checked that with my secretary. Of course, he still wants a copy of my passport, but with all the information he has by now he knows for sure that I am the right person. That's right.

"Dimitris has left you one of his properties, and I can assure you that it's a beautiful house. I'd like to come to an agreement with you regarding the settlement of the will, there's no need for you to come to Skopelos if you do not have time for that", he says diplomatically, "everything can be taken care of remotely nowadays. Please think about it for a moment. Your secretary provided me with your business email address, or would you prefer that I email you privately? I will send you all the details and the possibilities for settlement by email, so you can take your time and quietly think about it."

You probably understand that my adventure begins right there and then. An adventure one does not ask for; one that messes up your sense of order. I apologize, however the long introduction to my life was necessary. Otherwise you won't be able to grasp the meaning of the rest of the story.

Every day we hope for excitement and adventure. By now I know this doesn't apply to me, I don't want adventure. I do not want to push my limits. I just want to live my life as it has finally become calm and stable. I can afford anything, I own a beautiful collection of antiques, a beautifully restored farmhouse, have good friends and more than three million on my bank account. Seen this way: I've been successful in my working life and I'm proud of that. My success has more than compensated for my unmarried status and the resulting lack of grandchildren. My parents were proud of me and my success, and also glad that I didn't defile their existence with my homosexuality, I suspect. I truly believe they deserved that; I was very fond of them.

I sit at my desk with the Financial Times in front of me. I realize that the chaos has already hit me because I am unable to read the newspaper now. I simply sit there, while Dimitris' face slowly begins to appear before my eyes.

Dimitris

Dimitris, yes. I remember. I forgot to ask how he passed away, and quickly calculate how old he should be by now. I think he was three or four years older than me, he should have been sixty-three or sixty-four years now. That's young. He must have been ill.

I'm going back in time. Which might be confusing for you but I have to. Especially now. With Dimitris marching into my life again in the strangest fashion, I should explain how I met him long ago, and who he was.

Ronald, the guy with whom I shared a flat, taught me how to party and drink beer. He taught me how to laugh. Those were happy times. On Friday nights we went into town, later on Saturdays too. I often took the first train to my parents on Sunday morning, without any sleep, as not to miss the first church service. They resented me for this.
One evening, Ronald and I were walking on the Mauritsweg in Rotterdam. Ronald stopped at a

particular pub. He proposed to go inside but I hesitated; it was a gay bar. Ronald smiled, "You're gay and I'll just pretend." I can remember being utterly shocked. How did he know I was gay? And why did he still hang around with me? But I had no time to ponder, Ronald had already gone inside, so I followed.

In that bar, I learned that it was possible to be gay, although in relative seclusion. But I found it pleasant. At first I was afraid to run into acquaintances, guys from my village, but soon realized that it would mean that they would also have a lot to hide. So I felt moderately safe there.

I must have been around twenty-three years old when I first experienced gay love. It freed me in a sense, but it was also the start of a double life that I exposed myself to and would continue to do so. I went to that bar more often after that first time with Ronald. Ronald went along only twice. Later, I realized he must have put me on that track on purpose, to help me as the true friend he was.

Now that my secret was out in the open, my relationship with Ronald changed. I believe that I was constantly embarrassed in his presence and thus purposely deterred the friendship he wanted so badly. Ultimately, we lost sight of each other. I am so very sorry now, as it was important to me. I completely take the blame upon me. Perhaps my homosexual orientation has made me more or less autistic. I was unable to experience intense friendly contact with a heterosexual who knew that I was different. I dared not; I think it confused me too much.

I probably should explain myself here. Otherwise you might miss the point. Of course I felt like a man, a young man. And I led the same student life as all of my heterosexual classmates. Of course I wasn't crazy and could put everything concerning my sexual orientation into perspective. I just did not understand why a heterosexual person would want to be friends with a gay man. It made me feel ashamed and reluctant. I did not know what friendship truly was because, since childhood, I had a secret that on the one hand stood in the way of genuine friendship, and on the other hand, made friendship only possible as long as it was kept secret. When Ronald expressed that he knew, that he 'did not care with whom I had sex', as he once said to me, I suddenly felt so naked, sinful even.

Do you understand? I did not dare to walk through the house in my underpants, afraid that he would feel like I tried to make a pass at him. A reserve originated deep within me. And from what I know now, this reserve would play tricks on me during my whole life. A reserve that became prominently important in relation to my self-image. A reserve which meant that the secret life I was going to lead would leave me torn. I lived between delusion and reality. No one is able to keep that up for long, I know now.

I will continue my story.
I suddenly led a gay life, completely concealed for my family, my village and my church.
I met interesting people, men should I say. Went to wild parties, which were always private, and experienced being happy with my sexuality for the first time.
But on Sundays I sat in the church trembling. I had allowed a loving God within me now, but the reverend told a different story. And it didn't matter

how hard I tried; I kept having doubts about being right and thus kept fearing God's wrath.

I graduated. Of course I graduated. That was my sacred duty towards my parents. I never wondered whether the degree I obtained was what I truly wanted to do in life. My father wanted me to become an economist, to end up in the financial business. Many successful brothers from our church worked in that field. I still don't understand why and if there is anyone who should understand, it would be me. I always tell myself that working in the financial business grants power and power is important to carry out the word of God with authority. But I doubt that theory. I know many of the church members from my village too well to make them seem so negative.

After I finished economics, I started studying accounting and worked for a large company of auditors. I stayed there for at least a decade. After that, I moved to a bank's asset management division, and from there I worked myself up. By now I'm on the board of directors of the same asset management division and I'm good at what I do. When I write it down like this it certainly sounds very impressive, especially if I'd also mention all my privileges, bonuses and salary. I won't do that though. Because it's not impressive. I've worked in the same building for the last thirty years and have never allowed myself to experience a real adventure. So I do not understand how I could believe all those years that every day gave me new opportunities, and thus I hurried to the same building for the last thirty years, every day, with the same grand enthusiasm.

I think I was about thirty when I met Bart. He was antique dealer and lived on the Provenierssingel in Rotterdam. And there, on the Provenierssingel, is where I first met Dimitris.

Elizabeth sticks her head around the door with a so-called question, in truth she is simply very curious about my Greek acquaintance.
"Is something wrong," she asks, as I'm obviously staring off into the nothing in front of me, "bad news?"
I force a smile, because my private life is none of her business, even though she has been attempting to be my friend for the past fifteen years in addition to being my secretary, who understands me and would

like to cheer me up in my solitude. Just as she turns to walk away again, I hear myself asking her, to my horror, if she knows where the island of Skopelos actually is.

Sometimes I do not understand myself. Why did I just ask her that? Is it just curiosity, or do I suddenly feel a kind of incomprehensible interest in a man I met thirty years ago? And that's not even the real question I should ask myself. Get it out of your head Paul, I tell myself. But the damage is already done.

Liesbeth returns with an atlas, faster than the speed of light. I haven't the faintest idea where she found it. What are we supposed to do with an atlas here? She points the island out to me.
"You can also Google, Paul. You can find quite some information about the island. It is one of the Sporades."
She slides her right arm in front of me and grabs the mouse. I hate it when people do that, and I'm not even speaking about the intimate physical contact that results from it. I lean back as far as possible in order not to feel her body. Soon images of a Greek island appear on my screen. Beaches, terraces, a man

playing bazouki, women dancing in costumes, cats, chapels, olive trees.

"Gee, it looks like fun," Liesbeth says as she leaves me alone with the images.

My day is ruined. Nothing goes like I want it to anymore, like it usually does. All day I think back about Dimitris and memories keep flooding back. Actually, I want to go home, to search for old photos but I'm very dutiful and plough forth. I skip lunch because I'm not hungry anymore and Liesbeth, who apparently sees me struggling, remains scrupulously aloof. At three o'clock I decide it's enough. I want to go home, read the email from the notary and search for memories of Dimitris in my archives and in my head.

The Great Confusion

Obviously, you must be very curious about my meeting with Dimitris long ago. How long ago exactly? I wonder whilst driving my car on the way home. I will tell you my story, because I know now that my relationship with Dimitris has been important to me. Which is crazy, because just a few hours ago I had to think very hard before I could even remember him.

My brain is very capable of flawlessly avoiding irrelevant data regarding business matters, specifically containing emotions. I apparently erased Dimitris.

I met Dimitris, or Dimi as he was known to his friends, at Bart's during a party. I can see him very clearly before me now. Casually leaning against the wall. One hand in his pocket, the other holding a cigarette. He stood out because he was beautiful. Exceptionally beautiful. Not very tall, I was taller, but standing straight and proud and Mediterranean, with dark brown, almost black eyes. The way he looked at me was defiant and arrogant as well. What I later learned about Dimi was positive and negative at the same time, but arrogance was definitely not one of his traits. But that night he seemed arrogant to me.

We got talking. He told me that he had attended the Hotel Management School in Germany, and since then he had been working here and there. That he was born in the Greek province of Macedonia but he went chasing his sister to Germany. He asked about my work, where I lived, was extremely keen to hear about my budding interest in antiques and the reason I was hanging out with Bart at that time. Dimi liked to laugh. He showed his teeth when laughing. And as he talked about good food and nice things, he pursed his lips and made gestured with his hands. Later he told me that he was known as 'Mousie' by friends in Germany. And yes, when he pursed his lips, he resembled something of a mouse.

He also had more fun with the expensive antique glass he was holding, than with the wine Bart poured in to it. Dimi loved everything that was beautiful. I saw that immediately.

I enjoyed his company and I think he enjoyed mine. I've never been very good at recognizing emotions in others. My friends say I'm wrong, that I'm just afraid for feelings in general. Whether they're my own or someone else's. I do not know if they're right.

Anyway, that night I slept over at Bart's and so did Dimi. It will probably not surprise you that Dimi and I shared the same bed.

In the morning Dimi was already awake when I appeared in the kitchen. He made breakfast for us. He used Bart's finest china to cover the table, polished the cutlery and cleaned the glasses. Next to each plate was a tiny vase with freshly cut flowers from the garden. The sweet rolls smelled delicious. He squeezed oranges for us and poured the juice in our glasses, baked nearly perfect eggs, sunny side up with bacon. Only when everything was on the table, were we allowed to start eating. Dimi loved these scenes resembling a still life and wanted to enjoy the end result first, before it would be eaten. A habit that many people share who love to cook by the way. I see this on the Internet. They take pictures of their arranged plates. After breakfast we said goodbye. Why not? Gay men are not clingy, or so I'm told. I know better though. Still, they like to keep up appearances of absolute freedom and self-determination. Dimi asked for my address and phone number and I gave it to him. Bart looked skeptical and told me later that I had to watch out for 'those foreigners'. "Before you know it, he'll suddenly appear at your doorstep and you'll no longer be able to get rid of him."

Indeed, three weeks later Dimi suddenly stood on my doorstep. I didn't live in the farmhouse yet but had a nice apartment in Amsterdam, which I had redone by a stylist, a friend of mine. Here and there some beautiful antique pieces were strategically placed.

He didn't bring any luggage because he 'was staying somewhere else' but when I invited him to stay over later that night he had his bags in my apartment in no more than fifteen minutes. I never learned where he got those from in such a short time.

Dimi brought joy into my life, from the very beginning. He was caring and energetic. Respected my order of things, never changed anything, moved a chair or adjusted the layout of my closets. But he did bring color to my apartment. When I came home from work the next day, he had perked up the hall and living room with two gorgeous bouquets in vases equally beautiful. On my bedside tables in the bedroom he placed fragile silver vases, each containing a single fragrant rose.

In the evening I asked him how long he was planning to stay. I remember feeling embarrassed when doing so. It was slightly uncomfortable that Dimi was there so suddenly, but on the other hand I appreciated his presence very much. He would stay for only two weeks, because he had to return to Germany for his work. I remembered Bart's comment and his concerns and was a bit worried.

Perhaps I should explain a little here. It might seem like I felt embarrassed with Dimi's presence, which indeed I was. While simultaneously I was glad and happy to see him day after day. But also afraid that he would not live up to his word and stay longer after all. I've never talked about this with my friends, so I cannot give you their opinion on the subject. To understand these strange feelings I must rely entirely upon myself.

I think, no I'm actually sure, that I was afraid of open displays of homosexuality. Up until then, to the outside world I was just a regular single guy with a fulltime job. My homosexuality was something that took place behind closed doors entirely. I had no need whatsoever to change that. Because that was simply my life. To step out of that lifestyle would be a much bigger step for me than, for example, it would be for a heterosexual man who decides to move in with his girlfriend. For me it would mean a real transformation. Giving up a double life just like that. And I could not do that. From this I can only conclude that I did not accept myself, I found myself rather disgusting. But these are only considerations, which I didn't see until now unfortunately.

If were to discuss this with my friends, they would probably have blamed my parents and their faith in the church. I do not want to hear this though, especially since I doubt that is the real reason for the double life that not only I live, but many gay men of my age as well. It might be traced back to a time when homosexuality was not accepted, but in our time, in which there certainly has been some acceptance, our double life feels more like a way of life if I may say so. A way of life resulting from a certain inner hatred of ourselves.
Dimi and I have never spoken about a possible future for our relationship. That was irrelevant. We were in love and had fun, but I thought the fact that it would end in the long run was clear to both of us.

As I said before, Dimi colored my life. Every single day I was so happy to see him again after work. He cooked and to say he was good at it would be quite an understatement. When he started cooking, he would position all the vegetables and ingredients in the form of a still life on the kitchen counter. He found this to be beautiful and Dimi loved beautiful. He was energetic, caring and dedicated. But at the same time exceptionally egocentric and vain. Sometimes, when he felt he didn't get enough attention, he behaved like a spoiled little girl and could be cruel as well. Dimi had it in him to be very hard and relentless.

After two weeks Dimi departed, as promised. He left the house and all the vases empty. I was sad and relieved at the same time. But the void he left behind was painful.

So right now I'm on my way home from work. It's hot, I hate heat. Heat makes you sweat and I very much dislike sweating. I cannot tell you what I'm thinking about in the car. Confusion strikes me so intensely that I cannot even remember how long it takes me to get home. Even though I always record the duration of my journeys. A part of my fixation with numbers I guess.

Once I'm home, the confusion only gets worse. Normally I follow a fixed routine. I erase my voice messages, water the plants, dust and then pour myself a whiskey while checking the mail.
But I'm earlier than usual and the groceries have not been delivered yet, it is too early for whiskey and I feel an uncontrollable urge to search the attic for old photographs.

The two Pauls

I'm sitting on the ground in the attic, with some large boxes containing books and papers in front of me. I search through the boxes and when I think I have found the right one, I take it downstairs. At the big table, I spread out the pictures I find inside. And there he is; the first Dimitris, laughing at me. I somehow seem to have an endless amount of photographs of all the things we have done together. I recognize and remember everything at once. I feel no pain or sorrow though. Actually, I feel nothing. I look at pictures with petrified smiling faces, but they are nothing more than pictures to me. My lack of emotions scares me. Why don't I feel anything? And as usual, I do not understand myself.

This smiling man once was my great love. A few hours ago I learned that he passed away. But when I look at pictures of him, I feel nothing. It feels like I'm looking at a life that was never mine, at a love that never belonged to me. It worries me that I feel nothing, but at the same time this lack of feelings is actually welcome at this point.

In my mailbox I find the promised mail from the notary. He explains everything to me. I can accept the inheritance but also have the option to reject it. If so, I need to submit my reply by registered letter. But If I accept I don't have to do anything. He kindly informs me about the fact that, even though there is still no definite inventory of assets and liabilities, there are no debts whatsoever.

The notary also mentions the possible sale briefly 'in the case you attach no emotional value to the real estate' and gives me the name of a real estate agent on the island, with whom he has often done business and feels confident about. Finally, he also devotes a whole paragraph to the prevailing emotions. My big loss, the emptiness and so on.

So here I am. I have inherited a house that I don't want, in a country where it is too hot, from a guy I haven't seen in twenty-five years.

By now it's after eleven already. I'm still sitting at the big table. With a glass of whiskey in front of me. Not the wine I'm used to just before bedtime. No,

Whiskey. What's even worse; I placed the bottle next to my glass, simply because it feels convenient. What should I do? I feel so dizzy. What a horrible situation. I'm drunk, should go to bed, but still haven't decided yet. A panic washes over me... Dimitris has just waltzed into my life for the second time. For the second time, my whole life is turned upside down.

During the night I dream about him. We are together in Corfu: he looks at me from a rock as he poses before my camera. He looks at me, he looks at me and somehow he scares me. Then I wake up. It is ten to four, the alcohol has worn off. My head feels heavy, my mouth is dry. How am I supposed to go to work tomorrow, I wonder…

It is half past five. I'm back at my big table, smoking a cigar. The first cigar I've smoked since ten years. Shreds of the past flee through my mind, forgotten thoughts, pain I don't want to feel. The pictures I looked at this afternoon fly like a pendulum strung on a thread through my head. Flashes of light shoot before my eyes. The pictures become a movie. I look at them like I'm floating in the limbo between then and now. Dimi.

After Dimi's departure, we spoke to each other regularly on the phone. We wrote letters, cards. Sometimes he visited me during the weekends. I never went to Germany, he did not want me to because he did not have decent housing. He actually lived in the hotel where he worked. When Dimi came to the Netherlands it was quite the hassle, as Dimi didn't drive a car so he had to take the train. Because of his endless struggles handling a timetable, I always planned his trips. I tried to avoid situations where he had to change trains, because I was sure it would go wrong. While I still lived in Amsterdam all went well. But that year I moved to Asperen, where I bought a monumental farm. So if Dimi came over, I drove all the way to Amsterdam to pick him up. Dordrecht or Leerdam would have been closer, but he would have had to change trains once in the first scenario and even twice when going to Leerdam. Impossible.

The following summer, we planned a vacation together. He insisted on going to Greece with me. I agreed, despite my horror regarding hot countries. We went to Corfu, just the two of us, which was also a compromise. Dimi wanted to go on vacation with a few friends. Me? Not so much. I didn't know any of them and was afraid of wild gay scenes, which I surely did not want to expose myself to.

That particular vacation turned out to be rather nice and Corfu was beautiful. When I think about it now, it was actually great. We swam every day, lay in the sun, walked and drank cold white wine on shaded terraces. In the evenings we dined at different restaurants each night with delicious seafood. We bought pretty nothings. We had endless conversations about anything and everything. But never about us. Apparently I didn't think about it and neither did he.

Two weeks. Usually I can still remember little things from years ago that annoyed me, something I felt exceptionally opposed to but now, after all these years, nothing at all comes to mind. I got to know Dimi better and even though I despised his self-centeredness and vain disposition, I felt very connected to him.

It's five o'clock by now and I've actually made a decision. Two, really. I'll go to work tomorrow, since it will provide me with a welcome distraction. So I'll be a little tired; after years of dutifully taking enough sleep I surely have to be able to arrive in a somewhat less perfect state. My second conclusion is that I cannot decide whether I should accept the inheritance or not. I must go there to know for sure! I want to know where Dimi has spent the last twenty-five years of his life. I want to know with whom he lived there and how. I want to see his house, breathe in the atmosphere. Tomorrow I'll call my lawyer and ask for advice, but I am going to Greece, that's for sure.

You're probably thinking that this sounds very determined for an uncertain man like me; well you're right. But my decision to go to Skopelos has been taken after half a bottle of whiskey, great confusion and a mild panic. You will probably also ask yourself how it is possible that a doubting man can have such a responsible job as an asset manager. Asset management regularly requires the making of rapid decisions with minimal information. I know, it's contradictory. Let me explain. There are two Pauls colliding with each other here. The 'asset management Paul' takes rapid decisions about figures and business in general. He has a quick and sharp mind, can count well, numbers are more like words to him and he can quickly analyze potential risks in his mind. He is a manager of risk-taking and has always been excellent at it. The 'asset management Paul' knows the ropes, never uses a word too much. This Paul is calm and balanced, never intense or ambivalent. This Paul is loyal to his clients. He has never been ill and his behavior is acceptable to everyone; he is seen as a pillar of strength. This Paul is the Paul of the estate, the two cars, the big money and the antiques. This is the Paul who has nothing to do with feelings and emotions.

But there is a second Paul: 'emotional Paul'. I've got to know him recently and honestly find this Paul much nicer and more interesting than the first one. It took some trouble to get to know this Paul though. He was always latent but because he is so emotional and wavering, 'asset management Paul' hid him for years. I see 'emotional Paul' consciously for the first time this night after that bottle of whiskey. He is desperate because he has to take decisions without the logic of numbers. Because he knows nothing about feelings and is afraid of his own memories.
Asset management Paul decides to meet emotional Paul halfway. 'Go look at that house in that rotten Greece', he whispers in my ear and that's comforting.

The decision has been made. But that doesn't take the panic away.

No, I'm not schizophrenic! Be honest; everybody has a little piece within themselves that they would rather like to keep hidden. A small piece you don't really want to show to others. Most people barely even know their own bad sides. But I am quite familiar with mine; I'm gay and weak as well, as I never dared to openly express my homosexuality. But did I ever make anyone suffer because of this? Even sinners have a right to exist you know.
In my heart still lives the God of Love, who is gaining ground by the way. The weight of my sin, which made me live a life full of guilt begins to fade. Give it some time, and I might even become more human than many others.
The Kingdom of God that my father, mother and reverend told me about, really exists. I know now that it's easy to go inside, it's just a little hard to find.

You sure have become courageous Paul, after half a bottle of whiskey. Why are you bothering everyone with this long-winded story? You're an autistic fool, wallowing in your loneliness. You don't even notice how boring and tedious your story and your life are. What is this point that you are trying to make? Why are you so pedantic?

Oh dear, now it's going wrong. I do not wish to be pedantic. Is it not fair of me to try writing down the findings of my confusion? I feel as if it's important. Maybe just for me and not so much for anyone else. But something is going to happen, I can feel it, and that frightens me so much that I want nothing more than to float around in the pool of securities that, during the last sixty years, perhaps didn't make me very happy but carried me nonetheless until I slept. But now I cannot get back to sleep. I must go to Greece. That's all I know. And even the whiskey does not encourage me. I should go to bed and wait until tomorrow. Maybe it will all work out somehow.

After our holiday in Corfu we both remained silent for some time. As if we were shocked by all the pleasure and joy that we experienced those two weeks.

It was also strange: we parted at the airport. Dimi went his way, I went mine.

But we continued to call and write each other. From time to time he visited me in Asperen. We visited antiques fairs, galleries, museums. We ate in the best restaurants. We went shopping and to the movies. My life took place between the daily practice of asset management and the love of my life.

The alarm rings, I wake up in shock. For the first time in years, my alarm is faster than me. I experience difficulties going through my morning ritual. I feel tired. I didn't even iron a shirt last night or pick a suit. I forget the newspaper and there is no sandwich waiting for me in the fridge. The lemon I skip too, suddenly I'm in a hurry.

I arrive at the office but do not know how. The car radio is on, but I'm totally missing the essence of the conversation. Liesbeth fortunately waits the ten holy seconds before she storms into my office. I have obviously frightened her.
"Jesus Paul you look terrible!" She brings me my documents while she looks around nervously.
"Liesbeth," I try to sound as normal as possible, "can you figure out for me how I can reach the island of Skopelos, and call Ben for me please."
Apart from transferring me to Ben, my lawyer, I don't see or hear Liesbeth at all afterwards. At eleven

o'clock I have an appointment. At noon I'm finished for the day. Liesbeth comes into my office. She takes a seat next to me with a notepad under her arm. She doesn't ask me if I have time. She tells me that I have time. She should know.

"Listen Paul, you will need to choose between several options.

"If you want to travel business class, you can fly to Thessaloniki. You'll take a taxi to the port and then you have about six to seven hours of travelling left by ferry. I do not know if you have a decent connection, I could not find specific information but I will make some phone calls. It is also possible to travel by bus from Thessaloniki to Volos. That will take you three to four hours, after that you have another four hours on the ferry from Volos."

I look at her; "A bus?" She nods.

"You can skip that option," I tell her firmly.

Liesbeth crosses the particular option on her notepad. "Next one" she says, "you fly business class to Athens. You'll have to take a taxi at the airport to Piraeus. It's quite a drive but a taxi is comfortable. Your journey continues by ferry for about five hours." She looks at me quizzically. I make a gesture, implying she should continue. "The next option is the fastest but probably the most terrible for you as well." I hear a bit of mockery in her voice. "You will be flying a charter...," she shoots me a careful glance to monitor my immediate reaction, "...to Skiathos, where you'll take a five-minute taxi to the port, then continue by ferry for about one and a half hour. It depends on whether the ferry goes directly to Skopelos Town or stops at Glossa, another place on the island."

I sigh. "Can I rent a cabin on the ferry from Thessaloniki?"

"No" she says resolutely, "I already checked."

She tilts her head slightly to the side and looks at me with a grin: "I know you well, you know."

I don't give her the satisfaction of an answer, but instead let her delete the option that involves being on a boat for seven hours.

I choose the worst option: the charter. She smiles and teasingly gives me the option of a private jet and a helicopter for the final stretch. Apparently she doesn't even expect a reaction because she immediately stands up; "Are you sure? I'm going to book July seventh, there are not many places left."

I nod almost invisibly so she asks me again; "Come on Paul, a clear answer please!" She then holds out her hand and commands: "Credit card!"

I will not bore you with the details of the last seven days before my departure to Greece, the country I secretly detest. Well maybe a little. Those seven days were awful. My whole life was turned upside down, my sense of structure and order was lost completely. Every morning I woke up tired because I drank too much whiskey the evening before. My regular habits were an absolute mess.

I was confused. I was going to do something that I would normally never do, and yet I here I was. The days seemed endless whereas the nights were too short.

I made lists of what to take and what not, which clothes to pack. Did I even have shorts? Would I need a suit? And which shoes should I take with me; I didn't know if I would need closed shoes.

I tried to remember what I took to Corfu but there were no memories, nor any pictures of me which I could use as a reference for packing. Dimi never took pictures, although he happily allowed himself to be photographed by others. In those seven days before my trip, I slowly began to dislike the man who, for the second time around, threw my life upside down. Nevertheless, it was not enough to reconsider my decision to travel to Skopelos.

It all was what it was, and at the very least Liesbeth was very much taken with my decision. And even though she could not fore see what was going to play out there, she knew nothing of the inheritance after all, she was obviously pleased with my destination of choice. A sunny island, packed with tourists.

But let's move on to talk about Dimitris. Or, rather; Dimitris and I.

So after our holiday in Corfu we eventually stayed in touch, as I told you earlier. Frankly, nothing really changed. From time to time Dimi visited me in Asperen. He loved that house and the garden. He helped me with making a garden design and was surprised when I told him that I would have it executed by a professional gardener. More than just surprised, he was stunned when he heard what it would cost me. Dimi was good with gardens and plants. He designed the garden for me but I would not allow him to execute it. So he confined himself indoors for maintenance and odd jobs in the house while he was in Asperen.

When he was there, he was always doing something, working on something. He painted my kitchen, polished the stairs, and painted all ceilings throughout the house. Everything he did was near to perfection. Yet it bugged me from time to time: all that activity. When he was busy with a job around the house, he demanded complete control and accepted no objections whatsoever. Sometimes I was genuinely happy when it was Sunday and I could finally drive him to Amsterdam, to put him on the train home.

We never went on vacation together again. I don't know why. Corfu had been a success, but perhaps that was precisely the reason.

Sometimes we stayed together a bit longer than just for the weekend. In the fall I often took a week's leave, and so did he.

From time to time we went to Rotterdam to visit Bart. Bart now had these 'sliding-door evenings' and we were invariably invited to these events, amongst a few other chosen ones. Sliding-door evenings were a somewhat improved version of his wild gay parties.

After all, Bart was getting older too. His former parties were notorious in our circles. Then, at some point, he started feeling annoyed by this observation, while at the same time it became obvious to him that he needed more depth and meaning in his life. So Bart proclaimed himself as the protector of our culture. During these sliding-door evenings, his large living room at the Provenierssingel was divided in two separate parts: in front of and behind the sliding-doors. We were seated in the front part of the room. The seating was arranged in a way that turned all our gazes towards the doors. In case of a larger audience, some folding chairs were placed here and there. The space behind the sliding-door was a makeshift dressing room for, according to Bart, 'young and promising talent'. The sliding doors were a stage. And so we saw many young ballet dancers, musicians and singers appear between the sliding-doors. I must say that Bart did have a nose for talent and I've wondered more than once where he found all those pretty boys. After the performances there was always some dancing and feasting, with the usual possibility for using the bedrooms on the first floor for brief interludes.

Dimi enjoyed these evenings and so did I. It left me with some very nice memories. Not in the least because we were seen as a couple by now and thus the others spared us from unwanted advances.
That does not alter the fact that I was sure Dimi, apart from these evenings, did have a few covert affairs with some of Bart's regulars. Nonetheless, when I look back now, Dimi and I were actually very happy together. Happy and satisfied. Satisfaction is still the highest possible level of love, is it not? I loved Dimi and he loved me.

After three years, or was it four…? I don't remember exactly, but after a while Dimi announced, without at least carefully preparing me, without an introduction, without any consultation, that he would not come visit me anymore. He had accepted a position as a Hotel Manager in a hotel in Greece. I think that was the moment when he first mentioned the island of Skopelos, which is what confused me when the notary phoned me from that island. The name was vaguely familiar but I could not put my finger on it.
I remember that we were sitting on the couch. It rained. The water on the window distorted the image of the flowering cherry tree beside the terrace.

Suddenly that scene appears in my mind crystal clear. What a curious detail.

I was utterly speechless. A kind of long distance relationship had gradually developed between us but he ended it all so abruptly, as if it meant nothing to him.
I remember I was angry, bewildered; I felt betrayed. He tried to comfort me, put his hand on my knee and assured me that he would never forget me.
I could not predict what that promise truly meant for Dimi. At that moment I just knew for certain that Dimi had no feelings at all and tricked myself into thinking that it was probably better this way. It was over, the end. I now wonder whether Dimi had ever tried to talk to me about moving to the next, maybe more serious step in our relationship. Frankly I think he did, but because of my autistic and anxious disposition I never opted for a truly openly gay relationship.

I secluded myself afterwards. Stopped going to Bart's sliding-door evenings and threw myself into my work and my collection of antiques. Years later, when my mother died, I lived in a state of depression for some time as I wrote earlier. I experienced exactly the same sensation for the first time when I lost Dimi.

I took him to Amsterdam Central Station and there, on the platform, we said our final goodbyes. We shook hands and gave each other an impersonal slap on the shoulder like ordinary men. "Come visit me in the summer," he said. There was a slight hint of despair in his voice. I promised nothing.
It's probably clear by now that I have never visited Dimi on Skopelos and our parting was indeed, in the light of his recent death, very definite. I never saw Dimitris again.

If there ever was a chance for me to enter a committed relationship, to live together and, as is possible nowadays, to get married, it was with Dimi I realize now. I have never met a man with whom I have experienced the same unity and perfection as with Dimi.
As I write this I'm starting to doubt my honesty. Would I really have dared to confront my environment by openly coming out about my love for Dimi and therefore my homosexuality? Had I ever dared to do such a thing while my parents were still

alive? I am trying to invoke the feelings I had during that period. This proves very difficult and also feels like an unreliable source of information. People develop and change as time passes. I suspect that I was not aware of my own role in the breakup then and still held on too much to the belief that sin could simply never lead to happiness. In a way, that breakup was the equivalent of the destruction of something that was never meant to be and thus the ultimate form of self-destruction.

I basically proceeded with my regular activities and general way of life. In the years that followed after our breakup I became more confident thanks to my successful career, however, this also led to an innate fear that my bosses would eventually discover how I really lived my life. I believe I've always been aware of my own 'deficiency', if I may refer to it this way, because that is exactly how I experienced it. It was the ultimate form of self-hatred.

Dimi was gone and I had to move on. Gay relationships are different from heterosexual relationships. Being together and living together is not so obvious. At least that was the way it was then.

The current possibilities for gay marriage have changed this a lot and I think that's a good development. But that was not reality twenty-five years ago, so I got over my loss like a man and followed my own path. At the same time realizing that both Dimi and I had never really done anything else but go our own way. Even during our long distance relationship of three or even four years.
The question is why I rejected his final invitation to come to Skopelos, and furthermore, what would have happened if I had accepted it. I probably would have had to try harder to preserve what I wanted to keep. I think so, but I was guided by resentment and anger and I am, after all, a proud man. Furthermore, I was unconsciously convinced that my life was sinful and as such I didn't feel wholly entitled to experiencing happiness.

I have now described seven uninteresting days of too many drinks, too little sleep, worrying about what clothes to bring or not, which suitcase, which bag and which shoes. So I only would like to mention my last day at the office. Something happened which is not really relevant to my story, but I still feel it is noteworthy.

It's four o'clock in the afternoon when I feel an overwhelming urge to finally call it quits at work. My plane, that dreadful charter, leaves the next morning at the unholy and ungodly hour of seven in the morning. This means I have to leave at half past two in the middle of the night from Asperen to Schiphol Airport. So I want to be ready on time and go to bed early.

Just when I'm about to clean the last papers from my desk, Liesbeth sticks her head around the door: "You got a minute?" she asks. She doesn't wait for an answer as usual.

She stands before me, embarrassed, with her hands behind her back.

"I know you see me as an annoying busybody from time to time Paul. I know you think I'm being pushy and everything, but I just want to say that I really like working for you and feel very responsible for you. I want you to have a nice holiday and I'm glad you are going to that island." She pulls one of her hands from behind her back and holds it out in front of me. There's a package in it. "For you, Paul," she says, "but you cannot open it until you're already on the plane." I see tears in her eyes and want to hug her but

I am unable to do so as you know. So I thank her and express my appreciation for her in superlatives. This precise moment shows that she is a good secretary with an uncanny precautionary insight. It is definitely a sign, I see that now.

The Journey

It's July seventh, half past two in the middle of the night. Sleeping wasn't much of an option, and now I feel terrible. Exhausted I still try to follow my morning ritual. Apart from reading the paper of course, since it hasn't been delivered yet. With immense effort I stick to my normal routine, so last night I ironed a shirt and picked out some clothes for today. Indeed, clothes, not the usual suit. I'm not going to work so I'm not wearing a suit. Today I'm wearing soft corduroy pants, light brown, a soft blue shirt and a dark blue blazer, no tie. That should be an ok enough option, and not too hot either considering the weather. But I've packed a pair of linen trousers and a polo shirt in my hand luggage to be able to change, just in case.

I'm concerned about the taxi I ordered, hoping it'll be on time. There's also the possibility of driving my own Mercedes to the airport, but I find the idea that my car has to stay in a car park for three weeks rather annoying.

I eat my sandwich but I'm not exactly hungry. For a moment I ponder if I should seriously follow through with this plan. I can still change my mind. I comfort myself with the idea that I have some breathing room and can cancel the whole thing, well until I'm at customs that is. Apart from the reason for my trip, which is questionable at the very least, I find the idea of going to Greece utterly repulsive. In the financial business, Greece is certainly not appreciated. The top-heavy government, the prevailing culture of fraud and deception, the absurd retirement age of fifty-five years. It has cost our company a lot of money. I have no ties with that country and fear the decrepit state I will discover it in.

While I'm waiting for my taxi I realize that this whole enterprise cannot turn into anything else but a fiasco. Today I'm deliberately causing my own ruin, I believe. I try to remember my feelings from seven days ago. The fear of the events to come, and wonder whether that vision has not sprouted from my sick mind in order to have a legitimate reason to go. Then again, there's a huge probability that nothing will happen and I'll basically be stuck on an island for three weeks where I will be very bored and where I don't know anyone.

The taxi arrives on time and as a thief in the night I leave for a holiday I do not want, to a country that I do not wish to travel to.
The taxi driver tries quite hard to start a conversation with me but after several attempts he gives up. I'm absolutely not sociable and consequently a bit ashamed for my bluntness.

It is terribly busy at Schiphol Airport, despite this unholy hour. There are massive queues of people at check in, dressed in colorful shorts, dragging along their children carrying backpacks and stuffed animals under their arms. Everyone is cheerful but also pale due to lack of sleep. A man would never choose be here voluntarily, I think. Lost in the crowd, I await my turn and abhor Liesbeth because it was her idea. That's unfair, I know, but cut me some slack will you? Why should one always be courteous, good humored and friendly? I feel like insulting someone: anyone. Sorry, I'm certainly not at my best when I have not slept. And I've slept barely for a week by now.

When I have finally passed through customs, I decide I'm allowed to treat myself to a glass of whiskey,

since the wait will be long until I can board. I order a glass of orange juice!
That is the other Paul, the wise version: there is a war going on in my head.
At the gate, there's a long queue of tourists again. Temporarily released by their bosses, they rush to their destinations as if that is the only thing for which they live. I despise this type of hassle, flying business-class might have been better after all.

The atmosphere in the plane is good though. Apparently there are a number of families present who will celebrate their holiday together. Children are running back and forth and shout to each other across the headrests. Finally we're taking off. There is some fiddling with seat buttons going on and the ones above our heads. The Captain chips in over the intercom. People incessantly ask the hostess for this or that, who good-heartedly answers every request. Then there's also the food, the general buzz, the approving and disapproving comments and the shouting at each other again. And of course the highlight of the flight: the selling of perfumes and other trinkets. The flight only takes one and a half hours, so all of these mandatory components are finished consecutively at a killing pace.

There's a man sitting next to me. It's not clear to me whether he is traveling alone or has simply been seated in a different row than his wife and children. When I take the package out of my bag that Liesbeth gave me, he looks at me questioningly.
"Going on holiday?" he asks. I tell him that I'm travelling for business. With a nod, he points to the package: "From your wife?"
"Yes," I say and put it back in my bag.
"Don't you want to know what's in it?" he asks me again.
"I know what's in it," I lie and then lay my head against the window, pretending to go to sleep. The man seems to understand the hint and keeps his mouth shut for the rest of the trip. It is so lovely that certain people only need a hint to do what you want.

The descent of the plane is being started. Already? But we're descending for Kavala. That is the first stop. I look out the window and see a sunlit, but bare landscape. People stand up and rummage in the cupboards above their heads even though the space in the aisle is too tight for everyone at once. It is a bit of a mess and I cannot deny that I somehow feel weirdly comfortable in the maze that is now emerging. When all the Kavala-goers have exited the plane, a new batch of people is already coming back inside. These people are also Dutch but tanned. They obviously have just had their annual dose of sun. I get it now. This aircraft is flying in circles. In a moment, when I leave the plane at Skiathos, they will stay put and the plane will be filled again by people leaving Skiathos.

We leave and by now, I'm starting to look forward to our arrival. I'm a bit fed up. I find it incomprehensible that I endured those long flights to Rio de Janeiro, Buenos Aires, Cape Town and Sydney.

We are descending! Off to Skiathos. Below us I can see water, water and more water, even though the plane is flying terrifyingly low already. Where is all the land? And then, just as I'm preparing myself for a landing in the sea, the runway appears from underneath the plane. The Captain steps firmly on the brakes when we hit the ground, the people applaud;

terrible. Later, when I'm waiting on the ferry in the harbour I see the runway to my left and it's positively amazing. The start of the runway is literally where the sea ends and earth meets water.

We have to walk ourselves to the airport and to our luggage from the plane. I've never experienced this. Despite the terrible heat I'm starting to have some fun.

I go through customs, where all they really do is watch how a massive throng of tourists is making their way through the fences, then arrive at the luggage carrousel. The famous snatching. At the exit, like anywhere in the world, there are men and women with signs. I do not have to pay attention to the signs this time because I'm incognito, and that feels good. What a strange sensation, it's nice to be detached from expectations and waiting people. Feeling free… When I have grabbed my suitcase I move to the exit quietly. I do not need to shake hands with anyone, as previously stated, there is no one waiting for me with a sign. How delightful. To enjoy this freedom a bit longer I stop to explore a quaint little store without actually buying anything.

Through the exit, where Liesbeth told me to take a taxi, where are the taxis? I don't see any, though I notice a group of people who are standing on a curb, waiting in the blazing sun. A taxi drives up and, indeed, stops right there.

Nice, I think, and mingle with the people on the spot. The taxis come and go at a reasonable frequency. When it's my turn, the driver holds the door open for me and puts my suitcase in the trunk. Before I'm even sitting comfortably, three people start cramming themselves inside, a mother with two children sit down next to me and a man pushes himself diagonally in front of me.

"This will not fit," I say gently, "at least, not all of the luggage." The people look at me kindly.

"This is Greece" the man in front of me says while negotiating the fee of the ride. The trunk will not close anymore, a surfboard is sticking out. It's getting hot, very hot. But the man assures me it's only a short drive. I feel the thigh of the woman next to me pressing against my leg and an enormous sense of disgust washes over me.

The drive indeed turns out to be short like the man said and as Liesbeth also assured me. Only five minutes have passed and we're already driving into town. On one side, I see the port with many yachts and on the other side, terraces, terraces and more terraces.

Once we have arrived, I ask the driver where I can buy a ticket for the ferry but the man, who was seated in front of me, gives me an answer: "It's over there, follow us, we also have to buy tickets."

The ticket office is somewhat of a culture shock for me too. Three ladies are sitting behind three old iron desks, desks that would make a nice little profit in the Netherlands on the second hand market. The top drawers of the desks serve as a cash register and are wide open. Visible to everyone, they contain mountains of cash. The ladies certainly are taking their time. There is a Greek man in front of me, who is having some incomprehensible problem. The lady makes a phone call in his name, shows him some tables, points to something the map behind her. The man then seems satisfied and puts two hundred euros on the desk. He walks away. The lady pushes the two hundred euros to the side of her desk and starts helping the next person in line. While the small office has become overcrowded in the meantime, those two hundred euros are just lying there unprotected. The man suddenly returns, squeezing himself through the crowd, apparently making a joke because every single Greek person in the office starts laughing.

I buy my ticket: the woman speaks excellent English by the way. I have about one and a half hours before the ferry arrives.

"The ferry goes to Glossa first on Skopelos, don't get off there though, you won't be there yet," she said kindly.

What shall I do? I'm carrying my luggage with me so I'm not very mobile. It's hot and I'd like to change into something else. I decide to find a spot on one of the many terraces.

And there I am. A comforting peace slowly descends on me. The waiter appears quickly at my side. He smiles and begins talking in English to me immediately; "On holiday, sir?"

My god, I think; I must look like a tourist.

"Would you like something to drink, sir?"

"Yes," I say "a coffee would be nice."

"Do you want hot or cold coffee, sir?"

Why the hell would I want cold coffee? I ask him, but in a friendly way.

"Cold coffee is a delicacy in Greece, we call it 'frappé'. Everybody drinks it here." He points to some people on the terrace, "that's cold coffee, sir."
I see them drinking from their glasses with a straw.
"All right," I say "well I will have a cold coffee then."
"How would you like it, sir?"
"With milk and sugar, please."
"Would you like a lot of milk and sugar, or just about enough?"
"Keep it simple please and just to be sure, bring me a hot coffee as well, in case I don't like the cold version."
Apparently I amuse the waiter, he laughs.
"What kind of coffee would you like sir, Nescafe, filter or espresso?"
I'm about to ask what the difference is, but decide to choose the safe option instead and order an espresso.
Within a short time the waiter returns with both my cold and hot coffee. He also presents some kind of cake before me.
"I don't think I've ordered this," I say suspiciously.
"No sir, that is on the house, because it's your first time in Greece" and he laughs. "Welcome" he says, and he then disappears.

It's not my first time in Greece, I think, but I can't remember anything resembling cold coffee. Then I take Liesbeth's present from my bag. It contains a booklet: 'Everything about Greece'. How sweet I think, and browse through the booklet. I pause on page eighteen. The chapter is named; 'Coffee in Greece'. Liesbeth, how did you know...? And I try to suppress a smile.

It's hot and I'm tired, but the liveliness of the port and the lovely rattan sofa on which I'm seated give me a feeling of relaxation for the first time in weeks. The espresso is delicious and I suck on the straw of the frappe. I have to say, it tastes very fresh and delicious. Cars and motorbikes drive back and forth. Suddenly I'm hungry and beck on the waiter, who is talking to a man at the entrance of the café. He appears right away.

"I would like something to eat," I say. My questions are apparently too vague. The waiter smiles and probably wants to ask the same questions as before: do you want something cold or warm, do you want something large or small... But he changes his mind.

"Which ferry are you waiting for, sir?"

"Why", I ask, "is there more than just one?"

He points to the sea, and there, at the entrance of the harbor, I see a ship docking.

"That's the Cat. I assume you are going to Skopelos? The Cat goes to Skopelos, but there's also the ferry that goes to Skopelos in an hour."

"What's the difference?" I ask him.

"The Cat only carries passengers, the ferry also transports cars. The Cat is more like a water bus, sort of like the buses you have in the Netherlands."

I look at him quizzically. "Have you been in the Netherlands?" I ask him.

"Yes sir, in Delft. I studied something here in Thessaloniki that would be similar to civil engineering in the Netherlands, and was a guest student for three months at the University of Delft. You are from the Netherlands, right? In the Netherlands, civil engineering is focused on defenses against water, here in Greece it is the other way around, the prevention of dehydration of the islands. But show me your ticket, so I can see which boat you should take."

I give him my ticket and he smiles.

"You still have some time, this is not the boat you're supposed to take."

"Can't I just take this boat, like in the Netherlands, the first bus that comes?"

"No sir, the tickets are limited because there is limited space on the boats. The Cat is often simply full, in accordance with safety regulations. In addition, the Cat is much more expensive, it is a hydrofoil as you might be able to see, which travels much faster than the ferry."

I wonder why the lady behind the iron desk didn't offer me a ticket for the Cat. Probably because I asked her for a ticket for the ferry.

"You still have an hour so you can order whatever you want."

"Do you have something fresh, like a salad?"

"Of course," the waiter replies and recommends me the 'goriatiki'. "It's a Greek salad, very simple but fresh and tasty."

I order the Greek salad.

Once the waiter has left my table, I ask myself what this man, in his early thirties, who studied engineering, is doing waiting tables on a terrace like this.

The Greek salad is simple indeed. Chopped red onion, chunks of meat tomato, cucumber, black olives and feta. Oil, vinegar and some sort of herb, I think it's basil. Everything is served with fresh bread.

"Bon appetit," the waiter says in Dutch.

I look at him and smile, and somehow feel compelled to ask some questions about his studies in relation to his work.

"Work is currently a difficult subject in Greece sir. I have a wife and a child, my parents are old and do not have a lot of money. We all live together in Volos right now, which keeps our expenses low. During winter, I work there as a plumber and in the summer I go to the islands to work as a waiter. It does not bother me sir, the weather is nice!" and he laughs happily.

"Fortunately it is quiet today," I say.

"But not tonight sir, it gets quite busy in the evenings."

"You work here during the evenings as well?"

"I work from eleven am until... Well, until everyone is gone. Sometimes that's not until three o'clock."

"Then you work more than twelve hours," I say, surprised.

The waiter just smiles and makes a gesture, and then walks away.

The salad tastes very well. I dip the pieces of bread in the oil and feta and prick the salad on my fork.
Suddenly I feel like having a glass of white wine. As I turn to the entrance of the cafe, the waiter starts walking in my direction immediately.
"Skopelos is really nice sir, I was born there," he tells me as he puts down a small jug of wine in front of me.
My God, he probably knew Dimi, I think. I keep the conversation short this time.
"I will warn you when your ferry arrives," he says and disappears.

I could sit here for hours and am amazed that, despite the heat, I feel very comfortable.
During the next hour, I see more and more people seating themselves on the terraces. They are carrying bags, backpacks and suitcases. Many young people, dressed scarcely yet tastefully. They are wearing fashionable sunglasses. Some motorcycles appear, heavily loaded, as well as cars and trucks. They drive up the site of the ferry wharf and remain there, waiting in the blazing sun. I wonder if they all need to board the ferry and if so, that boat surely must be very large.

The waiter taps me on the shoulder and points towards the sea.

"Your ferry," he says. "But take it easy, it will take at least twenty minutes before it is berthed again."

At the entrance to the harbour, I see a huge ship enter the bay. It is truly immense.

As the ship gets closer, the activity on the dock increases. There are cars and pickups everywhere, dropping pallets with huge packages. Port officials take their places at the entrance to the wharf, police officers begin to regulate traffic.

I keep watching, fascinated by this chaotic bustle. Right in the front of the bay the huge ship turns, so its back will be positioned at the dock. The valves that allow all the cars to pass through go are already open, I can see the passengers waiting on the stairs. I pay the bill, thank the waiter, grab my things and cross the street to the ferry dock. I have to be extra careful due to all the hustle and bustle and for a brief moment, I resent those undisciplined Greeks.

At the entrance, I ask a man in a bright white uniform where I need to go. I imagine there is a queue somewhere between two fences, but the man makes a nonchalant arm movement followed by a nondescriptive 'there'. By now, a large crowd has formed with suitcases, bags and packages forming a chaotic mass on the docks. I see lovers saying their goodbyes, forklifts mingling with the crowd and putting packages on the dock. I join them, but we are pushed aside by police officers: there's a huge truck with a trailer turning into the narrow entrance of the port. When the ferry has moored, a red cord is removed that separates the people on the steps of the vessel from the docks. Like a fragmentation bomb, the ship spews its passengers. Everyone is walking in all directions, while at the same time cars are emerging from the center hold of the ship. The chaos is now complete. Port officials and police officers are diverting the traffic the best they can. I hate chaos, why is this whole scene so disorganized? Where are all the fences, lines and restrictions on the use of space?

The crowd, which, to my great displeasure I am now part of, commences forward. All these people want to board the ship. What seemed like a fairly organized group of people has now turned into a confused and impatient mob. An official comes over, asking for tickets. I do not understand this way of organization.

Curiously, the moving crowd remains standing on the dock, despite the absence of fences and rows.

At some point the ship is apparently empty. The man who checked our tickets only needs to make a brief gesture to get the crowd moving. There they go, with significant speed they all push for the hold, while left and right cars start driving onto the ferry too.

I get sucked into the crowd and before I know it, I find myself on a steep staircase.

At the top of the stairs, our tickets are checked again. I now find myself in a large, air-conditioned lounge. The room is filled with soft comfortable sofas in semi-circles around tables. People there are sleeping in every conceivable position, on top of and next to each other.

Others are playing cards. Women are playing with their children. There are TV screens in every corner. At the end of the room is a large bar where you can buy everything as far as I can tell. An official shows me a sign on the wall which says 'Skopelos', three meters further is a sign saying 'Glossa'. I am instructed to place my suitcase on a heap under the sign of Skopelos, I'm hesitant but do it anyway.

I definitely do not want to stay inside, so after dumping my suitcase I head for the first door I see. I go to the railing on the back of the ship and look down onto the dock.

The rows of cars are moving. The trucks have to board the ferry in reverse gear. It's precision work. The side mirrors are folded and men of the harbor are accompanying the drivers, 'right, left' they command, all while talking and laughing with the drivers. The truck and trailer below me start to move. Driving onto the tailgate, which is about as wide as the truck, is an art form in itself. I am fascinated by this spectacle. Such excellent driving skills. I now understand that some cars need to go first because we moor at two more harbours. All cars and trucks have to be in the correct order.

Slowly the huge queue of cars is shrinking, swallowed by the hold of the ship that seems to have an infinite capacity.

Bewildered, I note that this whole spectacle also runs smoothly without fences, lines and rows. We have been loading now for about twenty minutes and everything is almost on the ferry.

And there you have it. The dock is empty. The officials of the port and the ferry company are exchanging a few last jokes with the first mate, who has placed himself on some sort of balcony right below me on the stern. He is giving commands through a microphone. The cables are cast off, the ferry is leaving. The engines rumble.

Now would actually be a good time to tell you more about Dimi and I. So much has been happening around me the past few hours, things that constantly distracted my attention from you. I might as well take some time. I'm sitting on the shady side of the ship and looking down at the water, coming to the surface with the swirling motion of the propeller of the ship. It is blue, more azure. Slowly the port of Skiathos fades away. Which means now would be a good time to talk to you but then, something happens again.
The door swings open and a young lad comes out, with a pack of Pall Mall in one hand and a cigarette in the other. He looks around, sees me and sits down resolutely in front of me.
"On vacation?" he asks insolently.
It's the third person who has asked me the same question in just a few hours' time. I nod and smile as friendly as possible. Yes, I'm on vacation, I confirm to the boy. How surprising.

He offers me a cigarette, and although I do not smoke, haven't smoked for more than ten years, I take him up on his offer.

"Where are you from?"

I tell him that I am from the Netherlands. Because I do not feel for a cross-examination I'm going to ask him questions.

"I work on Skopelos."

"Oh," I say and ask him what he does.

"I am a waiter in Agnontas, do you know Skopelos?"

I shake my head.

"Agnontas is a small fishing village, at least that's what it was, now it's primarily home to seafood restaurants. If you have time to spare you should come and see."

"Where are you from in Greece?" I ask him.

"I'm not from Greece, I was born in Albania. But we live in Volos now."

"Albania?" I ask, surprised.

"Oh sir, there are currently many Albanians in Greece, mostly working here."

"But there is a lot of unemployment at the moment," I say.

The boy laughs, "It's even worse in Albania."

We chat for about forty-five minutes, he goes ashore in Glossa. While parting, he gives me a hand and tells me his name: Aggelos.

By now, it's impossible for me to talk to you again because I want to take a look at Glossa, the first inhabited sign of Skopelos. I want to take a look at the people boarding and leaving, I want to see the trucks.

When we are moored with the rear of the ship facing the dock, I find myself standing in the sun, but it does not bother me. I actually don't even notice the heat, fascinated as I am by the spectacle on the wharf. Glossa is located high above the harbour, stuck to the side of the mountain. A densely built-up area covered with white houses, with colorful, mostly blue window-frames. The port is called Loutrakie. I notice that people live here, there is even a bus stop at the beginning of the wharf. As in Skiathos, I see large terraces with rattan sofas and sunshades. There are people talking and reading.

I would like to have gone ashore to sit down and read too. That suddenly seems like a great idea. The surroundings of Glossa are completely green, with trees everywhere. It seems as if the island is one big forest. There are dozens of fishing boats in the bay, anchored and flowing on the waves. I see a yacht here and there. It looks delightfully peaceful.

Aggelos is waving at me from the docks. Even faster than on Skiathos, everything is outside that needs to be outside and inside what should go inside. The first mate reappears on his balcony. We leave. My eyes are still fixed on the island. I want to know where I am, why I haven't prepared myself more adequately, I wonder. During the next hour I keep seeing Skopelos on the right side of the ferry. A rock full of trees, it seems. Hardly any houses to be seen.
In a shady spot on the ship, I will now finally take the time to continue my story.

After saying goodbye to Dimi at Amsterdam Central Station, I was in shock.
First there was the grief, which was so overwhelmingly huge I believed it would never pass. All my days were gray and I had trouble picking up my normal routine. That was the first time I was absent from work for a week. But Bart scolded me out of bed. I needed to get it together, he told me. Dimi was not worth it. I never thanked him for that, even

though it was definitely an act of friendship. I already wrote that I erased Bart from my life at that point. That wasn't only because of him, but rather the memories I had in relation to him. Not until later, I understood that I should have faced those memories but I'm a coward, as you know. You know me by now, a bit of a shut-in and scared of feelings.

Then the anger came. Partly due to Bart's harsh words. Dimi was not that nice, really. He could be ruthless when it served his interests, hard and unapproachable. I consoled myself with the thought that it was better this way. All in all, I would not have been the right partner for him, I'm too accommodating and allow too much in a relationship. Of course, that was not the whole story. I was also guilty of being concerned only with my own life. Truthfully, Dimi's departure was a blessing. How was it expected to continue anyway? Would there really have come a time when I would openly come out regarding my sexual orientation, including all of its consequences? I do not know. At the very least not as long as my parents were still alive. But would I then have had the courage?

Somewhere at the beginning of this story I wrote that the way I dealt with my sexual orientation was a part of my personality, my character. Suddenly I doubt this. I think the dilemma of my life has indeed been leading, each time with the choices I made. My personality, my character, is rather the result of my sexuality, not the cause of my way of life. How terribly sad actually, when you need to draw such a conclusion at the age of sixty. Perhaps some of my friends are right when they blame society for their loneliness and their limited ability to lead a full and happy life.

Again, I do not understand what is going on with me, why I'm writing this. It seems like, here on this ship, I have found a different perspective.

After the anger came resignation. And that particular state of mind gave me the opportunity to pull myself back into my fort, where there was no room for sentimental matters and thus continue my successful career alongside my intimate secret life. Explaining it this way makes it sound split and extremely difficult. As if I committed adultery for many years, without

my wife knowing. But is that really a fair comparison?
In reality it was easy and relaxed, but the gap between emotion and reason became bigger and bigger without me realizing.

At the end of this period I had completely erased Dimi from my system. There wasn't even a slight possibility to think back to the lovely times we had together with something even remotely resembling a sense of pleasure. It was simply gone.
In that light, you should also see and understand the completion of my friendship with Bart. There was no room for relationships which reminded me of Dimi in any possible way. I hid all the memories of Dimi in the boxes I stuffed away in my attic.

Dimi called me twice and he wrote me three letters, which I obviously answered properly. This happened in the phase of resignation. Which means that his calls and letters simply arrived too late.

The green shores to my right continue to pass by. But by now, I also see bays and occasional clusters of houses against the side of the mountain. Between the trees, rocks and roads show up. I wonder how the view must be seen from the country, there in the shade of the trees. It's a curious thought. Apparently I want to be there and look out over the blue sea. I smell the scent of pine trees carried by a warm breeze. It makes me close my eyes for a brief moment, while I breathe in through my nose.

And then, suddenly, when I notice the small white church, standing out against the blue sky, on a cliff, I also see the town appearing from behind the rock. The boat turns gradually. Now I can see the bay, the harbour. The town, stuck against the wall in the same way as Glossa, is built in a semicircle around the bay. It's bigger than Glossa. From this distance I can already see the traffic on the docks, the people, the terraces with rattan sofas and colored cushions. Then the boat starts to spin in the bay. From my spot on the aft deck I see the wharf appearing, the mate has taken his place on the balcony again and is giving orders. Beside me people are pushing their way through the commotion. Some are waving enthusiastically to someone in the crowd below on the docks. People are coming from everywhere. I try to go inside to get my suitcase, but there's a massive crowd. There's nothing else to do but quietly await my turn.

Again, no sign of any organization, no queue, no clearly marked route. At the baggage place people are tearing and pulling at their property.

I go through the lounge, down the steep stairs, across the ramp and then I put my first foot on Skopelese soil. It is just after four o'clock. I have arrived.

The House

I told the notary I would travel to Skopelos, but I never told him when. So I decide to take a seat on one of the terraces and call him. But first I seem to have to deal with an extremely fast waiter again. "I would like a frappé, with a bit of milk and sugar please." I learn quickly.

The phone is ringing, someone picks up. I hear a woman's voice: "No, the notary is not present at the moment, but I can help you too Mr. van den Berg. We've been expecting you. Welcome to Skopelos! Did you arrive on the four o'clock ferry? Unfortunately I won't be able to meet you right away. Do you have a place to stay tonight? If it's ok with you, I'm going to do the following. First I'll book you a room in a hotel, at our expense of course. Where are you exactly? I'll call you back in five minutes. Is the number I'm seeing on my screen your number?"

I sink back into the cushions and once again I'm very comfortable. As promised, my phone rings exactly five minutes later.

"Mr. van den Berg, I booked a room for you in hotel Aeolos. You will be picked up within half an hour, by a car with the name of the hotel on the side. I told them you are sitting right across the ferry dock, on the terrace with the yellow pillows. The hotel is not far from where you are, you can easily eat something in the village tonight if you'd like. I can meet you tomorrow at ten am, if that would be a suitable time for you?"

I offer to visit the notary's office myself tomorrow, if she can provide me with an address, but she laughs; "You will never find it, Mr. van den Berg. Not all of our streets have names, plus it is really very complicated to find anything here."

I don't even get the chance to finish my frappé, when a car with the hotel's name appears. I wave to the driver. He approaches me, gives me a hand and grabs the suitcase next to me.

The hotel really is just a short drive further down the road.

It is a fairly large hotel with a driveway and a plateau. Once inside, I am immediately welcomed by a lady behind the counter. She writes down my personal information and walks me to my room herself. It is a room with a balcony and air conditioning.

"If you want to use the air conditioning, it is advisable to close the balcony doors," she tells me. "Do you want me to switch on the air conditioning for you?"
I thank her kindly, I'll just open the doors. I want to see the view. She leaves me alone.
I stand on the balcony and look straight onto the harbour. The ferry is still there. I take a bottle of white wine from the minibar in my room and sit on the balcony, there are two chairs.

While quietly sitting there, I notice there aren't many thoughts coming up in my mind, but I feel a great weariness instead. The fatigue is so intense that I decide to lie down on the bed.

I lie on the big, soft bed. I have taken off my clothes. In my head, Paul tells me I should shut the balcony doors and switch on the air conditioning. But the other Paul refuses and whispers 'it's lovely this way'. I sink off into a deep sleep.

I wake up suddenly, startled. It's getting dark. When I look at my watch I see that it's almost ten o'clock. Suddenly I feel rushed. I would very much like something to eat, but it might be too late for that already. I take a quick shower and put on some light clothing from my suitcase. I'm down in the lobby at half past ten and ask the lady behind the desk if I can still grab something to eat around here. She looks at me, surprised; "Of course sir, that's possible all through the night if you want." Reassured, I go outside.

It is busy. People are strolling on the docks, arm in arm. The closer I get to the village, the busier it becomes.

The wharf, which was still open to traffic this afternoon, is now closed so the pedestrians can move about freely. A few police officers are standing next to the roadblock. The terrace I was sitting at this afternoon is completely full. There is a large TV screen that I apparently overlooked earlier, it's showing a soccer match. From time to time indistinct agreeing, disapproving or joyful shouts emerge from the terrace. Women are eating ice cream, children are running and chasing each other between the tables and chairs. I stroll along with the crowd. There is a carriage with little bells for rent, apparently. There's also a man with a mule, a little girl is currently riding it. She looks excitedly at her father and mother, who are walking beside her, while the driver is leading the animal along the docks. There are several stalls around the area selling things like jewelry, fruits, olives, sweet corn, soap. A boy is playing his guitar on the pavement, he has a tray in front of him containing a few coins. I am now walking along the middle of the docks. On my left side I can see endless terraces, all serving satisfied customers, on my right I have the sea with fishing boats and yachts. Some are up for rent according to the accompanying signs, the owners are standing on the wharf trying to sell their wares: you can make trips to other islands, see dolphins and visit beautiful beaches. At the very end of the docks, I see the same church that I first saw this afternoon, before the ferry turned in the bay and I suddenly saw the town. It's been built high on a cliff, a staircase leads upstairs. Behind a wall in front of the church I can see a priest in a black robe, with that characteristic black hat on his head.

I want to explore that chapel up there, but then remember that it might become a little late to go somewhere to eat so I settle down at the last restaurant, at the very end of the docks.

Actually, I don't exactly settle down. Right when I want to walk up the terrace I'm greeted by one of the waiters.

"Would you like something to eat, sir?" He leads me to a table near the entrance of the restaurant. I don't see any tables inside the place. The waiter sees me looking and invites me to come inside and decide what I want to eat. The interior is nothing more than a large kitchen. He points me to the fish and shellfish, the mousaki, souvlaki, the saganaki. Chefs are cooking right behind the low display. I am greeted kindly. A bit shy due to the attention, I quickly pick something and buy myself a jug of white wine. When I return to the entrance, my eye catches a picture on the wall. A huge freighter is depicted on it. In an instance, an old man appears next to me who was sitting near the entrance with a drink just now. Now he's standing beside me. He looks like someone who always smiles.

"That was my ship sir. I sailed on it for twenty years. Where do you come from?" he asks me.

I tell him that I am from the Netherlands. His eyes begin to twinkle. "Oh, sir, the Netherlands, I have been to Rotterdam so often that I know it better than most Dutchmen!" He points to the kitchen behind the display case: "Those are my sons." Two lads in the kitchen give me a friendly nod.

"When I finished sailing I went back to my island, got married and started this restaurant. The two waiters outside are also sons of mine." He looks proud. Rightly so, I see four young men, all four equally handsome. "Now I'm pretty much retired and let them do all the work."

He pats me on the shoulder. "There's your wine, have a seat." He shakes my hand and introduces himself as Aggelos. It is the second Aggelos who introduces himself to me at the end of a conversation. He repeats my name as if he wants to burn it into his memory.

At half past one I leave the restaurant and walk back to the hotel in a slow pace. I think about Dimi, who must have walked here regularly during the last twenty-five years. Where did he live though? Tomorrow I will know.

Once I'm back in my room I sit on the balcony for a little while. I drink a second bottle of white wine and enjoy the night. I don't really enjoy silence though, the village is clearly still a long way from going to bed.

This newly found peace I feel inside. I would like to take a moment to talk about it. There's something strange going on. Today was a day that I did not ask for, to all intents and purposes. An excruciatingly early start, the charter flight, a cab crammed with people, hordes of people on the ferry, the overall chaos. Today was a rollercoaster for me. And yet I feel satisfied and peaceful. While thinking back, the faces of the two Aggeloses appear immediately as well as the waiter in Skiathos who is also a civil engineer. People make contact with each other easily here, without having to talk about their job and status first. That's nice, but it's also strange that I find this enjoyable.

I have traveled the world. I have been to Cape Town, Sydney, Perth. I visited London, Paris, Berlin and Barcelona. I flew to New York, Miami, Chicago, Tokyo and several other places I can't even remember. Yet all of this, the hassle I experienced today, it is completely new to me. How can that be? I wonder. I have already been in similar environments and situations. So why have I experienced this day so intensely?

Before you started reading my story, I obviously read the story again myself. I somehow noticed, that I'm being sucked into a funnel, unintendedly and unwantedly, without really noticing, one that I cannot come out of. Is the Judgment of God near?
I'm out of wine. Another day filled with above average alcohol consumption. I don't really care, I'm going to bed.

It is half past nine when I sit down for breakfast. The breakfast room is simple and cozy. I'm the first one present, but slowly the guests start arriving. By half past ten the room is entirely full. Breakfast is rich and tasty with lots of orange juice, boiled eggs, feta, fresh white bread and jam.
I feel rested, then again, I had a fantastic night's sleep on a soft bed under a cool blanket. I didn't put on my silk pyjamas. Paul slept in the nude tonight.

I walk into the lobby at ten o'clock sharp and there, sitting on the only sofa in the room, I see a woman. She looks at me quizzically so I walk towards her immediately.
"Mr. van den Berg?" she asks. I nod.

"Paul van den Berg," I say. Again I seem to learn fast. People introduce themselves to each other by first and last name, but immediately switch to a first name basis. I do not know whether this is a Greek custom, in any case it must be Skopelese. She invites me to sit down. She must be about thirty-five years old, a little chubby but with an exceptionally friendly disposition. She wears her thick black hair in a ponytail with large sunglasses on her forehead.

"I am very sorry that your friend Dimitris has passed away, Paul. He was a special man. I knew him well personally.

We were all very shocked. How did you hear of his death?"

Immediately I feel exposed and ashamed.

"Catherina, it's the notary who initially informed me. I have not been in contact with Dimitris for the past twenty-five years."

"Oh," she says "then the fact that you were informed about his passing so bluntly is even more regrettable. The loss of contact between you both doesn't influence the inheritance though. The will is still valid."

"How did he die?" I ask her.

"He had a heart attack while he was alone. He was found by his friend on a Thursday. We think it must have happened on Wednesday, because he did some shopping in the village on Tuesday and apparently still had the time to eat his supper. At least, that's what the medical examiner in Larisa stated."

Now I feel extremely uncomfortable. Catherina sees that and proceeds quickly by explaining the procedure. She looks at me encouragingly, but will obviously not compromise her professionalism by emotional involvement.

"I wanted to show you the house first, afterwards we can go to our office to settle everything. I've booked the hotel for one night only. If you would like to stay a while longer, you will have to take care of that yourself. This night was at our expense. But I can imagine that, if you accept the inheritance, you might want to stay in your new home. It's up to you, of course." I remain silent.

"Shall we go? Or would you like to have a cup of coffee first to relax a little?" she says, as she puts her hand on mine.

We step into a small KIA and drive away from the docks again, then turn left at the corner where the village begins. We drive a bit further down a wider street, at the end we turn right. The road goes upwards and appears to be a circular path to reach the higher part of the village. I look around me, it is busy and lively everywhere but I feel dejected. Once we're at the top, the KIA turns right into the village. The street is about as wide as the car, there's only just enough space. It's amazing that cars are even allowed to drive here but Catherina is resolute. The pedestrians we encounter push themselves against the walls of the adjacent houses as we pass them by. Then she stops. She parks the car next to one of those walls in a narrow side street, it won't be in the way of other traffic. I notice there's no traffic in the narrow street itself, because it quickly turns into a stone staircase. A woman is coming down the stairs with a plastic bag filled with fruits in her hand. Catherina exchanges a few words with her. The woman looks at me curiously and gives me a friendly nod.

"Here it is," Catherine says, pointing to the building on the corner. It's a traditional Greek building, with white plastered walls, though the window frames are not the usual blue or yellow but made with well-lacquered wood. I don't exactly know what belongs to the house and what doesn't, since I've never been in a similar house before. There is a door downstairs, but Catherina takes me up a flight of stairs to the side of the house, which leads to the first floor. She opens the door.

I wish I could relive that moment. I wasn't attentive enough and now I can't remember what I was thinking, or feeling.

We are in a small white hall with a wardrobe. There is a box in the corner that immediately catches my attention. It is antique, Greek antique to be precise.

To the right is a staircase that leads upstairs, the stairs straight ahead lead downstairs. I walk into a room, there's a large bed to my left, a bench and table on the right hand a circular brick fireplace in the corner. This room looks warm and cozy, albeit a bit dark.

"Dimitris put this house up for rent in the summer, which is why he created guestrooms on both the first and on the second floor" Catherina explains.

There are two windows facing the street side. The room is very spacious, I'd give it about thirty square meters. Old wooden planks cover the whole floor, which have been lacquered beautifully. There are small carpets on the floor here and there. The stairs lead us to the next floor, with a room about the same size but much lighter. Besides the two windows, it has a French balcony. The interior is tasteful and warm. There's a wooden floor with rugs scattered around the space as well.

We then go all the way downstairs and arrive in a large kitchen which is slightly below street level. To reach the street you have to take a few steps up the stairs, where you will reach the door that I saw earlier.

The kitchen is simple but sleek. The washing machine and dishwasher are placed in a niche. On the opposite side of the kitchen, a wooden bench has been nailed to the wall including a table and a few chairs around it. In the corner on the street side, a round fireplace has been constructed. The bathroom and toilet are both accessible through the kitchen. The bathroom is quite modest, with a shower and a sink.

This concludes the description of the house. I feel like a realtor.

I do not want to make the impression that I'm inspecting my newly acquired possession, or estimating its value. You know, see if it's good enough. I don't know exactly how to present myself to be honest. Actually, I'm only interested in the idea that Dimi lived here, walked here, cooked here. I'm still looking for feelings within myself. But I feel nothing, sorrow nor regret, there is only silence. Nothing at all. I still don't understand why Dimi has favored me in his will.

Catherina has taken a seat at the kitchen table and is drinking some water from a bottle she brought with her. She lets me move about, but I'm done soon. I don't want to inspect the closets or open any drawers.
"Sit down Paul," she says. "It is quite difficult to separate my work from the emotions I feel because of Dimi's passing. But if you would like me to, I can tell you a little bit about Dimi."
I'm in doubt; do I want to know it all? Yet I nod.
"Yes, please go ahead," and I take a seat across from her at the kitchen table.
"Okay" Catherine says. "Dimi came to Skopelos, the moment he became the manager of the hotel you stayed at tonight."
I am shocked and Catherine notices.
"Didn't you know?" she asks, startled.
"I knew about his new job, but I didn't know the hotel."

"Sorry," she says, "I thought I was doing you a favour."

"It's okay Catherina, you didn't know."

"I do not know, of course, what happened between you two and don't have to know either."

"Nothing happened, really. When he started working here, he wasn't able to visit me in the Netherlands anymore and in a way, our relationship sort of ended on its own." I look at her and see the relief on her face.

"Yes, that's similar to what I've heard," she says.

I feel the blood drain from my face. "What do you mean by that?" I ask her suspiciously.

"You're the Paul with the big farm and antiques, right? Dimi often spoke of you, especially the past few years. I believe he loved you very much. He pretty much compared everyone to you, no one was ever good enough. He told me about your holiday in Corfu, about your visits to museums and the Netherlands, he spoke about cultural evenings at a friend's house in Rotterdam. He also told me about your farm and garden; he absolutely loved it. I think he secretly hoped you would visit him here at some point..."

It has become dead quiet inside me. It's as if I am no longer able to breathe, to see, to hear. But my hearing is fine, for I hear Catherina tell stories about Dimi and me, stories I had forgotten until a week ago. I hear her say that Dimi loved me. Until a week ago, I did not even know anymore that I loved him too.

Because I can feel now, feel too much, I cover my face with my hands. Dimi spoke about me. Dimi had not forgotten me. Dimi loved me… Catherina strokes my hand, but keeps on talking. Live through this Paul, live through it, I tell myself.

"He turned the hotel garden into something wonderful. When the previous owner sold the hotel about five years ago, Dimi quit because the new owner wanted to tear down the garden and as you might have seen; he has indeed done so. Dimi then started his own business. He already owned two houses in the village, this one is one of them, and he then built an additional four houses near Stafilos in traditional Greek style, along with his brother in law and sister. Do you know where that is? I'll show you on the map, in a moment. Everything Dimi created was beautiful.

He brought all his German connections here. People he met during his studies or relations he formed through his sister and brother in law. His sister lives in Frankfurt. He knew Dorus the Baroness, one of the first regular tourists here on the island. Ivan Rebroff, the singer. Dimi loved to gather important people around him with high social standing. I did not see him as being predominant himself. How did you perceive him, Paul?

The baroness is deceased, Ivan too. They scattered his ashes in Agnontas. You didn't know this, Paul?"

I shake my head and still have my eyes hidden behind my hands.

"Shall I look if I can find some coffee? I'll make you a cup." She rummages in the cupboards for a while, finds coffee and places two cups in front of me on the kitchen table. They're beautiful cups, a kind of golden mother of pearl. Truly something Dimi would own, I think.

"He was talking about you more often lately. He told me that he wanted to visit you in the winter. I didn't take him too seriously, because he told me he also wanted to buy an apartment in Volos 'to spend the winter months'. I think he felt lonely. He had narrowed coronary arteries. The doctor sent him to the cardiologist, but he never went. He didn't take his medication. Sometimes I think he deliberately let it come this far..." I hear a sob in her voice.

A bomb has exploded in my body. I want to scream but my throat feels like it's locked tight. I want to wave my arms around but I'm paralyzed. I want to cry but not a single tear appears. My body is a desert. Everything is dry and dead. I am desperate. I feel guilt and it weighs heavy on me.

"How do you know Dimi," I ask her, when I seem to have regained some control over my voice.
"Oh, as a schoolgirl I worked in his hotel for two seasons. Dimi was very loyal towards his relations. Later, when I bumped into him again after a long summer season, he spread his arms, gave me a huge smile, kissed me on two cheeks and then said 'you are getting fat.'"
She giggles, "Dimi could be cruel, very cruel. For instance, he hated my husband. He didn't even try to hide it either. Nothing about him was good enough: too short, too dark, too stupid, name it. But if we needed him he was always there, even for my husband."

We're drinking coffee in Dimi's kitchen. I am pleasantly surprised by Catherina's frankness, she's a nice woman.

"Did Dimi have a relationship?" I ask her while trying to keep my voice as normal as possible.

"Yes, he had a relationship but that was more the work of his friend Yorgos, who did everything for Dimi. He never said anything nice about Yorgos to me, while Yorgos really is a sweetheart. Dimi was very cruel as I already mentioned. By the way, it was actually Yorgos who found Dimi that afternoon.
It would be good if you could visit Yorgos one of these days. He will be very grateful. Dimi told Yorgos a lot about you as well. He is the chef of Restaurant Perivoli, you can expect great food being served there. I will pinpoint its location for you."

We sit in silence for a while, facing each other. My sorrow is immense. I feel powerless over these emotions. I don't want them. They frighten me. What will I do now? I feel lonely and wonder what the hell possessed me to come here. My trip to this island was doomed to become a fiasco; well, that's certainly coming true.

"Paul," Catherina said gently as she touches my hand. "What will you do? Will you accept?"

"Yes," I say, "of course. How can I say no? But I'm not sure whether I'm keeping the house."

Catherine slowly pushes the keys towards me.

"Here," she says "stay here for a while, without me."

"Should I not sign somewhere, or something?" I ask but Catherine makes a gesture.

"This is Skopelos Paul, I'll call you tomorrow." She kisses me on my cheeks. I'm not fast enough to avoid it but don't really want to either. I can feel a connection has formed between us, in that short hour we spent together in the kitchen of Dimi's house. It amazes me that I already feel so much at ease with this woman.

She turns around, just before she opens the door. "Dimi rented this house in the summer, he had a closet where he always put away his personal belongings. You can find the key on the keyring with the other keys." Then she leaves and I am left alone.

Never, never before in my life have I received such miserable news.

At first I am I crying for minutes. I don't know where these tears are coming from so suddenly, but there they are, pouring out incessantly. My whole body jerks, the sobbing prevents me from breathing. How awful, how awfully hopeless. The guilt that slowly arises feels violent, and unbearably heavy.

My hands are shaking. What should I do?

I search through my memories to find some long forgotten wise words from a friend that might help me now, but I find no words of comfort. I wish I did not feel like this, I can handle everything but not sadness, for sadness hurts unbearably. I don't want pain. If I had not travelled here this wouldn't have happened. I would have been somewhere in Italy right now, spending money on antiques and fine dining. In the company of friends, drinking wine...

I'm so tired. Where can I rest? Not in the house that Dimi owned, nor in the hotel that Dimi owned. Where can I find peace, I need to find peace...

The couch in the kitchen is too short for me but I try to make myself comfortable on it anyway. My legs are aimlessly hanging in the air. I support my head on the pillow. It smells like Nivea and feels soft in my neck. It feels good, lying down. I stare at the ceiling and imagine how Dimi must have been painting here, the way he did at my place. With white paint splatter in his dark hair, wearing plastic gloves and an old shirt. Dimi laughs at me, he is happy and so am I. I kiss him on the lips. It is a kiss of gratitude, simply because he's there.

I groan and feel a heavy cocktail of regret, sadness and loneliness flowing through my throat. It takes my breath away once more. Dimi.

Do you understand any of it? Real desperation is so hard to describe, especially for someone like me who has trouble even understanding himself. But my despair is very real. There are people who choose to undergo this, who do undergo it, not fight it. I think that's brave, I'm not so brave. I realize I have to try and set everything straight in my mind, so I can understand myself again and be at peace with this feeling. I have to undergo this.

Slowly, the chest convulsions subside. The tears stop rolling down my cheeks. But everything feels dull; my body, my life.

How is it even possible that two people misunderstood each other so gravely? Now it's too late. I can never make this right again. It must have some sort of deeper meaning, I believe. There must be a purpose to all of this and if there isn't, I will think of one myself.

I'm sitting up straight again. I want to go outside, not be alone any longer. Feel the sun, hear the people.

It's hot outside. 'Just keep walking down', Catherina told me, 'you'll always end up on the docks eventually'. I do as she told me and find myself in a maze of alleys and stairs. I see potted plants alongside the houses, women are knitting on the pavements, cats are washing themselves on stone walls. I find myself in an equally narrow street but without stairs. To my left and right are shops and suddenly I stop, I smell something. I smell something I have not smelled before and it's delicious. When I look around me, I see a gate that leads to the entrance of a church. It is a kind of alcove in the narrow street. Over the wall, that separates the street from the courtyard of the church, I see a lush jasmine bush hanging down. Thousands of flowers are filling the narrow street with a sweet odor.

"Greece has a distinctive scent," Dimi once said. "Greece caresses all your senses. Flowers Paul, that's why I love flowers so much, they add fragrance to one's life."

That I can even remember this surprises me. It was on Corfu that he told me this. "Find that scent and you will find happiness."

I am walking more slowly now, I have no idea what time it is, but suddenly I'm standing on the docks. It's the same corner where the boy was playing his guitar yesterday evening. I see the small white church on the cliffs in front of me. I want to go there. I want look my parents' God in the eyes, let him know that I'm still here, that I am alive and will live on. I want to tell him that I never should have listened to all that moralistic talk. I want to tell him that such nonsense actually makes people unhappy. And thus, I will also tell him that I will never again pray to a god who perceives me as sinful. The dock is still quiet, I calculate that it should be around four o'clock by now. But time is not important today and so I walk towards the stairs.

When I pass Aggelos' restaurant, where I ate last night, I hear someone shout my name. I look and see the old Aggelos. He gets up from his chair and waves at me.

Aggelos is sitting at the same table as he did last night. He is in the company of five older men now. Aggelos beckons me and invites me to the table. I'm surprised he remembered my name and accept his invitation. He gives me a hand and pats me on the back. He also introduces the other men to me. One of the handsome sons comes out and put a small glass in front of me. Aggelos pours ouzo into it without even asking. He lifts his glass. The others join. The men at the table don't speak English but nevertheless turn their attention to me from the beginning. They talk to me using cheerful hand gestures. They feel no embarrassment and accept no language barrier. I laugh about their antics, Aggelos translates in English wherever possible.

So here I am, burdened with the greatest sorrow of my entire life, struck down by terrible despair, angry at the God of my parents. I feel like a bad person and still these men offer me their happiness. I could cry, if it wasn't for the fact that these men make me laugh uncontrollably. I feel welcome and happy. My god, what is going on inside my heart?

For a split second I look up at the church. We are not finished yet…it echoes in my head.

Just after six o'clock the group of old men splits up. Men kiss each other here. Did you know that?

I stroll along the docks towards the hotel. I have decided I'm going to grab my things. I will now empty the cup completely.

Tonight I will sleep in Dimi's house.

Xenia and Lefteris

My belongings are brought to Dimi's house by car from the hotel. When everything is in its rightful place and I've looked at the bed on the second floor and opened the balcony doors, I leave the house again.

It's about time I ate something, I tell myself. But I actually don't want to stay in this house for much longer. I'm scared of the emotions I felt this morning. It makes me wonder whether the choice I made, namely to sleep here, is not just another form of penance and self-flagellation.

I wander through the old town after dinner. It really is charming and beautiful. The narrow streets, the stairs. Through the open windows and balcony doors, I hear fragments of conversations and music. I smell flowers, basil, rosemary, grilled fish; the smells alternate.

I encounter people on the staircases between the houses, as well as dogs, that are obviously on their way somewhere. Although it is late, I see children playing under the watchful eyes of old men and women, who are sitting on walls and pavements and talking to each other.

It's still warm, about twenty-eight degrees.

In the lower part of the village, the shops are more plentiful in the narrow streets. I find a shop with gorgeous Italian menswear, and there is even a store where I find some beautiful antique religious attributes. I see ladies' fashion shoes, jewelry. I do some shopping in a small supermarket: butter, Metaxa, wine, water and some sweets. I also want some cheese. I point to a piece of cheese in the cabinet that looks familiar. "What is that?" I ask.

"That's Koeda, sir."

Suddenly I see the official Dutch Gouda mark on the cheese. "Gouda," I correct him. He laughs, "No sir, Koeda."

It is half past one when I put the key in the lock and awkwardly fumble for the light switch. I put the groceries in the kitchen, take the Metaxa upstairs and take a seat on the balcony. Between the roofs of the houses I can see a tiny bit of the harbour below. It is a bright night, I see thousands of stars.

Dimi, I think, I'm going to empty the cup, I promise. I will face myself, no matter how much it will hurt me.

Can you understand my emotions? Did you see it coming? I definitely did not see it coming. I'm not particularly good with feelings. I'm not soft, neither am I sentimental. One of my qualities is that I can hide away hurt and grief so easily. I can't even manage to write about it. So I will try to describe my feelings in general, maybe that will make it easier for me.

When it became evident that Catherina already knew me and I learned that Dimi talked about me, it felt like I fell into a dark pit. It felt like a trap. I was overpowered by an immensely great fear and that anxiety made my tears flow. At least, I think that's how it went.

While sitting here, I wonder where that fear came from. What was it that I was suddenly so afraid of? I have to try to answer that question, because it will allow me to see myself. I have to do that, I just promised it to Dimi.

I start to ask myself all sorts of questions while trying to answer them. Even though, deep inside my howling brain, I know where the fear came from. I'm just too cowardly to admit it.

I feel disappointed in myself. That I never had the courage to openly profess my love for him. Worse even; that I never openly came out for my sexual orientation.

It is unstoppable by now, waves of emotions overwhelm me. I'm so terribly incapacitated. How do you do it; facing yourself? I'm fucking sixty years old but not able to show normal human behaviour. How could this happen, that I lost myself? Or maybe never found myself?

I go into the room and open all the cupboards I can find. I want this done before I go to sleep. But everything in here is related to tourism: flyers of Skopelos, timetables of the bus and the ferry.
Phone numbers: of the doctor, the pharmacy, the taxi.

So now I have to get into bed, Dimi's bed. I just wish I will be able to sleep, and won't be haunted by dreams.

It's nine o'clock when I'm woken up by the noise on the streets. I make fresh coffee downstairs, take a shower and dress myself. I remember I saw a baker at the docks, so I go there and buy myself some bread. While going back to Dimi's house, I get lost. But once I'm at the right height, I follow the parallel road and find my way home.

At 10:00am Catherina calls.

"I'll come and pick you up Paul, where are you? At Dimi's? Oh I'll be there in five minutes."

Catherine arrives within five minutes. The office is apparently nearby. We leave immediately, because 'the notary is there and wants to meet you'. Indeed, the office is near. I couldn't have found it myself though.

Nothing in this notary's office is similar to a Dutch notary's offices, with their beautiful marble entrance halls, the art on the walls and tastefully decorated offices.

Here, it looks like the furniture comes from a flea market and the office hasn't been painted in twenty years. There are two areas. Behind the entrance is one room. It's where Catherina is sitting, it is also some sort of kitchen where coffee can be made. Next to it is the second room, which is the office of the notary. It is about ten square meters. An old sofa has been positioned against the wall, a desk opposite the sofa. It is difficult to see how the desk really looks, because it is stacked with mountains of file boxes. Along the walls are shelves, bending under the weight of the files. On the desk are also piles of files. The notary shakes my hand, he is dressed in linen pants and a shirt with the buttons open all the way down to his belly. Black chest hair protrudes from the shirt. Suddenly the phone rings. Well, I can hear a phone ring, but can't actually see one. The notary then digs under a mountain of papers and picks up the phone. With the phone to his ear, he motions me to sit down. I sit on the couch and observe the room with amazement. So this is where the most powerful man of the island sits, as Catherina refers to him. Powerful, because he knows about everyone's property, powerful because he knows where people fight over property, especially over land 'as this is a farming community', Catherina told me. Catherina is his eventual successor. But she fears the position, because she doubts her ability to cope well with such power.

After the phone call the notary approaches me. He shakes my hand again and introduces himself. My god, his name is also Dimitris.
He explains to me how the procedure works. He signs a document of five pages with countless stamps and seals. It is written in Greek. Then he leaves. He gives me a pat on the shoulder and is gone.

Catherine translates the document for me.
"When you sign, a lawyer needs to be present. That is the law in Greece. So you cannot sign now, we would need to call a lawyer first. The notary has already signed, which he also should have done in the presence of the lawyer, but hey, this is Skopelos," she says, grinning.
I understand that this is some kind of transfer document. If I sign, Dimi's house will be mine.
"When would you like to sign, Paul?"
"Make an appointment with the lawyer, who pays this guy anyway?" I ask.
"It's your lawyer Paul. Representing your interests so you pay, and it's a woman."
"I want to sign as soon as possible, so please make an appointment with her."

As she promised me yesterday, she takes a map and points out the location of Jorgos' restaurant Perivoli, as well as the place where Ivans' ashes have been scattered, Agnontas, and where Stafilos is.

"Paul, Dimi's sister and brother in law are on the island. They know you're here and would like to meet you." Catherina looks a bit gloomy when she tells me this. I feel somewhat reserved. After all, I have received a part of their inheritance. Who knows; maybe they'll feel discredited in some way, or they could use the money themselves.

"How do they know I'm here?" I ask.

"I told them. I think it's good if you go there. They are nice people and they don't blame you for anything as far as I know."

Catherine gives me a phone number: "Speak German Paul, they don't speak English. And I recommend you to arrange a method of transportation for yourself by the way. You won't get everywhere by bus. You can rent cars, scooters and motorbikes on every street corner. I'll call you as soon as I have made an appointment with the lawyer."

I walk by Dimi's house to pick up some money. It's still early and I want to see more of the island today. I buy a map of the island at a kiosk. Then I go to the bus station which is easy to find; it is next to the ferry dock.

I'm lucky, the first bus leaves in fifteen minutes.

There are some people waiting, the bus doors are still closed. The driver is sitting behind the wheel while eating a sandwich.

After ten minutes the driver opens the doors and the horde of people plunges forward towards the opening. It's like no one believes they will get on the bus without pushing.

What a show, I think, and distance myself.

I'm one of the last people to go inside.

It is a bus with two seats on both sides and a narrow aisle in the middle. It is crammed; people are sitting on each other's lap on some chairs.

The driver doesn't sell tickets. The remarkable system of a vendor is in place here. When the bus starts moving a man, who is much too fat for the job, starts to squeeze himself through the people with an iron ticket box on his protruding belly. He wears shorts and a shirt he left open unabashedly.

All those scantily clad bodies so close together. Yuck, I think. I will rent a car first thing tomorrow.

The bus drives out of the village but I can't see much due of the amount of people standing, falling to all sides at the slightest steering input from the driver. The first stop is Stafilos, or at least that's what the driver announces. A lot of people get off the bus here, packed with bags and towels. The bus is climbing up, to my left I can see the ocean and the view is nothing short of spectacular. Seen from above, the sea looks like golden foil that sparkles in the sunlight. Here and there I can make out tiny bobbing sailboats, looking as if they're not making any progress in that wavy sea.

The road turns away from the sea and drives into a forest. We are constantly overtaken by scooters and motorcycles left and right. Cars make dangerous manoeuvres while overtaking the bus. We then drive down and make a sharp turn to the right. Everyone in the bus tumbles down again. Over people's heads I see houses appearing.

'Agnontas', it sounds through the microphone.

How do I get out now, do I have to squeeze myself through the people? I tell the people around me that I want to get off. To my relief, all standing passengers in the bus get out of the bus for me to allow me passage.

The bus has stopped on a broad quay where fishing boats and yachts are moored. Agnontas is next to a bay with a U-shape. One long side of the U is the quay where I am standing, on the other side I see my bus driving up and away among the trees, which means there is a road there. At the bottom of the U there is a row of restaurants, less than a meter from the sea. Here and there are some piers reaching into the water in front of the many fishing boats. On one of the piers, I see squids hanging to dry. At the end of this picturesque row there's a beach, with tables and chairs, and there is a big tree on the beach with dozens of people sitting or sleeping underneath it. All terraces are covered snugly against the sun. I take a seat on one of the terraces.

I hear someone say 'Paul' while simultaneously receiving a pat on the back. It's the other Aggelos, from the ferry. "Nice man, that you're here, did you take the bus?" He laughs "You have to rent a scooter man, that bus is terrible."

I order tzatziki, calamari, octopus prepared with vinegar and garlic, bread and of course white wine.

I see people swimming, the water is clear and blue. So clear that I can see the bottom of the boats lying at anchor; it's as if they are floating.

After dinner I call Dimi's sister, we agree to meet up tomorrow at their place.

As I read back what I've just written, it looks a lot like a tourist brochure. That's remarkable; you would almost think that I'm enjoying myself.
Let me put it this way: I am definitely not bored. After yesterday, with all the emotions that flooded through me, I feel much better today. I slept well and have accepted the events that occurred yesterday. It's just the way love goes. So many people break up. It's not my fault that Dimi has never forgotten me. The fact that I never visited him was my own choice and I still support my decision upon reflection. I am sorry if he felt abandoned, the feeling was certainly mutual.

Everything is back in place, everything feels rational again. Reason has prevailed. I'm proud of myself.

I have decided to stay at Dimi's house during the rest of the holiday. The house suits me and I consider it a tribute to the man I forgot. It's the least I can do.
The house is genuinely pleasant. I have started to search through the cabinets. It might sound a little greedy, but I just want to know what is hidden and

stacked away. There are some nice antique pieces here and there and subsequently I noticed that Dimi tastefully combined old furniture.

I'm finished on the second floor. I've researched everything and even discarded some objects. I don't know why, I'm not going to keep this house after all. After my holiday I will put it up for sale. I will donate the proceeds to charity in Greece, which is also a kind of ode to Dimi because he loved the country where he was born so much.

I'm going to take some larger steps now. To describe every minute of every day is boring and not very relevant to my story. But there's one thing I would like to report.

I rented a scooter! Not a car, but a scooter! It suddenly seemed much more enjoyable, and less hot too. I drove the scooter to Agnontas again and while driving, I got one of those scent experiences again. The forest smelled so nice of pine trees. I think that scent will forever be linked to the spot on Skopelos where I noticed it for the first time. Dimi was right when he told me that Greece has its own scent.

I've gone all the way to the northern tip of the island and finally ate something in Glossa under the sunshades, watching the bobbing fishing boats.
With my self-prepared sandwiches, I went looking for the church of Agios Ioanis where the last scene from the musical Mama Mia was recorded, and visited the comfortable beach of Limnonari. I drove into the mountains behind Skopelos Town and visited the magnificent monastery Evagelistrias. There are still three nuns living there. All three of them very old. I also found an ancient spring along the way where I quenched my thirst with fresh clear water.
I spent hours sitting on a terrace high above Panormos, overlooking the beautiful sea. In the distance, the vague outlines of other islands were visible. Every day I bought fresh bread at the bakery on the docks and tried to resist the delicious pastries, but failed. I bought my groceries in the small supermarket of the Koeda-cheese. I like that man. On the road to the top, I found a shop selling fresh fruits and vegetables. You can buy one potato there and even pick it out yourself. I also bought two onions, fresh mint and delicious fruits.

As agreed, I will go to Dimi's sister and brother in law. His sister, her name is Xenia, explained to me how to find my way to their location. I am nervous. Xenia sounded nice on the phone but whichever way you look at it; I'm still stealing a part of their inheritance. Or at least it feels that way.

Xenia and her husband live in one of the houses of the resort, as far as I have understood. They built it together with Dimi. Dimi ran it while they stayed in Germany most of the time where they apparently lived for thirty years. It is supposedly located somewhere parallel to the road to Stafilos, though higher against the mountainside. They refer to the unpaved road as 'the old road to Stafilos'. That doesn't leave much to imagination. Once I'm up there, I need to give right of way to a flock of sheep and their shepherd. After that I turn right, and continue for about three hundred meters, as Xenia told me. It is situated on the left side.

I see it right away once I pass it. Xenia has described it very well. The gate is open, and an elderly man is walking towards me. He is wearing a pair of shorts and a linen shirt with short sleeves. It hangs loosely around his shoulders, untied. He looks somewhat surly. As I park my scooter he gives me a hand and looks at me intently.

To my left and right are the four whitewashed cottages that Dimi built.

The frames are made of wood. Since the houses are built against a slope, each one has a flight of stairs leading to the entrance on the first floor and covered terrace. The first floor is level at the rear.

All walls are covered with plants, large bougainvillea's and oleanders blooming profusely along the walls of the houses. It all looks well-groomed and lush.

A woman emerges from behind the plants now. She has a watering can in her hand and it strikes me at this distance that she moves the same way Dimi did.

Then she's in front of me and shakes my hand. Her eyes, the shape of her face... A shiver passes through me. It's as if, after twenty-five years, I am looking into Dimi's eyes.

Lefteris takes the lead, we walk behind him to the last house and while he talks, I try to look around me. We are all a bit reserved.

He walks in front of me on the steps, until we arrive on the terrace: there is a large table in the middle with four chairs. On the edge of the stone wall surrounding the terrace I can see sticks, shells and stones, neatly arranged, just like in Dimi's house around the two fireplaces.

"What are you drinking, Paul?" Xenia asks me.
She is small and slender, almost fragile, but also attractive. She is wearing a strapless cotton sundress.
"I'll have water," I say because I don't consider it to be the right time for coffee, it is too hot, and find it inappropriate to ask for something stronger.
"Water? Come on, the weather demands a cold white wine or beer."
Lefteris now turns towards me: "I'm a beer-drinking Greek, I could have a beer with you?"
I agree with a beer. Lefteris leaves the terrace and walks down the stairs. Xenia also leaves and goes inside.
Lefteris comes back with four half-liter bottles, he is planning something I think. Xenia comes back with glasses and a bottle of ouzo.
"I do not drink beer, it makes me pee a lot," she says.

"Do you know what happened?" Xenia asks me and without waiting for an answer she starts talking.

"He had narrowed coronary arteries but refused to go to a cardiologist, he didn't want any pills. I called him on the twenty-ninth of April but he didn't pick up, we were in Frankfurt then. I called him six times, it was nothing like Dimi not to pick up the phone. Then I called Yorgos, but he was in Volos. He promised me to check up on Dimi when he would be back on Skopelos in the afternoon. Yorgos saw him through the window in the bathroom."

She stands up and beckons me to come over to the window, indeed you can see into the bathroom a bit from that spot.

"This is not the house where it happened though," Xenia tells me. "I wouldn't have been able to get a wink of sleep in the house where he died." She points: "It happened there. All these houses are identical." Yorgos immediately called the police. Dimi fell down and hit his head against the sink; he had a head wound. We have seen the police photos. We think he really suffered, laid there gasping for breath. The autopsy revealed that his coronary arteries were completely clogged. It probably happened on Wednesday morning while he took a shower: Dimi always showered in the morning. Thursday afternoon Yorgos found him, around half past five."

"I am so sorry," I manage to say.

Xenia continues, "He has often spoken about you Paul, but you haven't been in contact anymore, I believe?"

"No," I say. I take a sip of my beer and notice that Lefteris is observing me.

He joins in the conversation. "He was a stubborn man, didn't take his pills, denied his illness. I have always had a somewhat difficult relationship with him. We have done some things together, this resort for example but now we have to live with the consequences. Everything should be divided among the heirs. He also has a sister and a brother, but half of all is ours. There is strife in the family."

He looks exasperated. I ask him if everything has been documented.

"Yes of course, but not which houses are ours. We will have to buy out the family but it is still a hassle. Don't misunderstand me Paul, we don't mind that you've inherited a house, we are happy for you as it's a nice house in a good location, but his sister in Athens is certainly bothered by it. She is making our lives very difficult while we remain here maintaining the whole place."

The ice is broken by now. We talk about Dimi, about the hotel where he worked, the garden and Skopelos. I tell them about our relationship a long time ago and how it ended. I realize it's the first time that I speak about Dimi and me, about our undertakings, his visits to the Netherlands. I tell them about his odd jobs in my farm, his stubbornness and quirkiness. I basically tell them everything about my love for the man who I saw for the last time thirty years ago. It feels good, it's like the story has been tucked away somewhere deep inside my brain, waiting to be told. The words come to me naturally.

For the first time in twenty-five years I tell my story, our story. The pictures I found in my attic at home, how they showed me fossilized memories which are starting to come alive, flow. Our past is becoming real and is back in my head, like a part of me, like a part of my life.

It's so strange. These people know that was I their brother's lover. Yet they listen attentively. I feel no judgment at all. They ask questions and even enrich my story with their own anecdotes. I was not prepared for this and it gives me the feeling that Dimi and I were real for the first time, that Dimi and I were really a couple. Everyone here knows about me and

Dimi. I can even talk about our relationship freely. I can... And it feels good.

Lefteris and Xenia have been living in Germany for thirty years, where they owned a transport business, but sold it by now. Lefteris is seventy-three but he appears youthful in his activities. Xenia is sixty-eight. She reminds me of Dimi in everything: her eyes, the shape of her face, the way she moves and talks with her hands. Xenia is the type of woman who will always remain a girl. She chatters at a stretch. And when she walks, she actually hops. Lefteris looks bothered by her from time to time. I can hear him sigh.

For a moment, I look at him after such a sigh. He winks at me.

I like these people.

"Paul," Xenia says at the end of the evening, "next Saturday is Name-day in the Irini chapel close by. Come with us."

I look at Lefteris; "What is a Name-day?"

"Greeks do not celebrate their birthday on their birthday but on Name-day. Almost all Greeks are named after a saint and most saints have a Name-day. It is celebrated throughout the community. Sometimes a party is organized, sometimes there is only a small service. There won't be any partying here at the chapel of Irini, but a service will take place."

I do not feel like going to church but Xenia is not the type of woman you refuse something. I think Lefteris understands me. He chuckles.

"I'm not religious," Xenia tells me, "but it is considered important to be there. A lot of people will be present, it's a nice way of seeing each other again."

"In Greece, many people joined the Greek Orthodox Church," says Lefteris "which doesn't necessarily mean that all of them are extremely religious. But our church is very much embedded in our culture. If you'd like me to Paul, we could meet up one night and I could tell you a thing or two about Greeks. They don't exactly have a good reputation in Germany at the moment, or in the Netherlands, which is not entirely justified."

I'm excited about his invitation and accept it gratefully.

"Next Saturday I'll be sitting next to you, so I can explain to you what is happening. Don't worry, it's not even similar to a church service as we know in Germany and the Netherlands."

We say goodbye around half past eleven. Xenia wraps her arms around me like I'm the prodigal son and kisses me on both cheeks. Lefteris shakes my hand, pats me on my back and kisses me as well.
I step on the scooter and hope that I will get home safely. It is pitch dark outside and the road isn't paved.
These people have caressed my soul. It's like they are family to me and also genuinely like to give me that feeling. I'm so glad I got to know them.

At home I pour a Metaxa in the kitchen, put on a CD with Goethe songs from the closet here and pick up the pieces of wood lying on the mantelpiece. These bits of wood have probably been in the water for a long period. Some of them are roots, other pieces are clearly carved wood from crates or boxes. Because they have been in the water for so long, they are soft and round, the veins are visible to the eye.
Goethe; the fairy king and sticks from the sea. A curious metaphor.
I'm savouring my Metaxa.
I opened the exterior door in the kitchen, so the sounds from the street can mingle with the music occasionally.

It gives a pleasant kind of lively peace.

I could talk to you now, but why should I. You know more than me. Am I enjoying myself now according to you? It feels like the iron band around my heart has loosened its grip. Not that I was I ever aware of that band, that happened here, on the island. But I can feel it now. And yes, I am enjoying myself I think.

Now, after a week I already have my own spot at the kitchen table, where I put my things: papers, Ipad, those kinds of things.

Upstairs on the second floor, where I sleep, I placed a chair and a small table on the balcony. I'm pretty sure I will take a moment to sit down there briefly before I go to sleep.

I like the scent of Skopelos on my balcony. I saw a shop where they sell plants this afternoon; I'm going to buy some basil there tomorrow to put on the balcony.

I did not think the heat would have so little effect on me. During the days I eat on covered terraces and drink white wine in the shade, in the evenings I usually take a stroll into the town and enjoy the warmth and scents that I smell everywhere.

The people are very much ok. Actually, I have only met nice people up until now. Soon I'm going to talk to Lefteris about the Greeks, which I like. I want to get to know them. I want to know this country. I want to find the nuance.

Today, I've pulled up a chair at Aggelos' old men's table for the third time already. I don't understand that I wasn't afraid to do so, but I did it and was greeted like an old friend again. Tomorrow night I'm going to look for Janis' bar here in town. That was also a friend of Dimi's. Xenia and Lefteris have advised me to go to that bar.

Who am I

I am wandering on a Greek island. I don't know why, nor do I have a destination. I still cannot believe I'm here. But since I arrived here, I have been reliving those years full of struggles.
I have often pondered on the value of my existence, for myself, for others, for the world, for the people around me.
It has suddenly become an Odyssey and I feel exactly like Odysseus. On my way home, although that's a seemingly unattainable goal. The gods are not well disposed towards me and make my return impossible for many years. I will remain a wanderer.

For a very long time I genuinely believed that someone like me has lesser rights to such a home. Because that is simply what I have been taught. I was a sinful man. Not because I was punished with homosexuality, but because I also gave in to my sexual orientation. That was the worst sin. I should have worn my divine punishment and continued the rest of my life as a sad monk, resigning from all pleasures regarding sensual love. That is not what I did though. For many years, I was convinced to be a sinful pervert. But as the years have passed, I have come to doubt this hypothesis and this doubt slowly sparked unrest as well as desire somewhere in my body. I wanted to live in freedom, to love and be loved. Is that not the only true message of Jesus, love?

And one day I just dropped everything. I had to go somewhere I really did not want to go. I still don't understand why I did this. What is the meaning behind it all? What is the point?

Is it truly possible to transform the figures I use to speak into words, gestures, caresses?

Is it possible to be the person I denied being for sixty years?

Is it really true that there is a God of love who challenges me to be who I truly am?

I sit in the kitchen of the house that was Dimi's only a few weeks ago, but now somehow belongs to both of us.

It is evening and the only source of light in the house is the lamp above the table. I can feel its warmth on my head.

I have a pile of letters and cards in front of me, which I found in a cupboard in the kitchen. They're my letters and cards. I wrote them to Dimi and he put them away neatly, arranged by date.

My hand rests on the stack, carefully tied together with a piece of string. I should read them but I'm scared.

The heart which has had so much to endure cringes at the thought of anything I ever wrote to him. I can remember some things, I'm not afraid of those. I'm afraid of all the words that I forgot.

I untie the piece of string and start reading.

I read everything by order of date. First the cards, then the letters.

My god. So much love. Why did I banish that from my life?

Suddenly I feel very alone.

I understand everything now. It was I who did not understand the heart. It was I who let myself down. I was the one who left me. Not Dimi, I myself. Again I cry, I can taste the saltiness of my own tears in my mouth.

The blame that struck me like a sudden bolt of lightning when I was sitting at this table for the first time with Catherina, and that same blame I managed to park so neatly in the no man's land of margin just a day later, pushed away from the real text, away from the words that matter. That blame is back now. I cannot deny it anymore. Is this morbid hatred or intense love Dimi, what are you doing to me? Where are you sending me to, what more do I have to experience until the cup is empty?

I don't know where all of this ends and if I will ever be able to find what you want me to look for.

Slowly it is becoming clear. This holiday will indeed be my downfall as I already predicted. A fiasco, because I am learning but do not know how to put theory into practice. The loneliness I feel is bigger and blacker than ever. How do I get back to the world where I have always easily found my way? I forgot to smell, I was color blind, senseless and cowardly. My life was similar to a gravel path: hard, cold and lumpy. My own gravel path, five meters long.

Dimi, I visited your brother in law and sister and came to love them.

I sat at Aggelos and his old friends, we drank ouzo and I came to love them.

I visited Janis at his bar with the marvelous view of the harbour and the beautiful music. And I came to love him.

I went to eat at Yorgos at his restaurant Perivoli, where devotion and serenity make a person happy.

I visited Agnontas where Ivans' ashes bob on the waves of the clear blue water and I started to love it.

Did you know that I had such a big heart Dimi? I certainly did not. I didn't even know I was able to do and feel in such a way.

I have decided not to talk to you all anymore. You probably consider my emotional awkwardness a joke, and that makes me feel ashamed. Moreover, you already know where this ends, while I do not know yet. From now on, I will only talk to Dimi. I think he deserves that.

The cup must be emptied

It is Name-day in the chapel of Irini today. I am meeting Xenia and Lefteris at their house at a quarter to seven. The service starts at seven.
Lefteris told me the chapel is situated on private land and that the owners have been maintaining the chapel for generations with much dedication.
Because church services make me a little nervous, I decide to drive by the chapel in the morning to take a first look.

The chapel isn't hard to find. It is on the same old road to Stafilos but a bit further ahead, more towards the village like the place where Xenia and Lefteris live.
It looks beautiful from the road. It is placed higher than the road though, you have to go up six steps to get to the chapel and because many people are at work right now, I choose not to. I'm afraid it might be seen as bold.

The chapel is tiny. Seen from the road, it doesn't seem to be larger than ten square meters. Where all those people will be seated this evening is beyond me. There are also some garlands attached to the small chapel, with flags containing written messages, I recognize some phrases from the Bible in Ancient Greek. The wall around the area, as I am now accustomed to, holds dozens of pots with plants and flowers. This place smells too, Dimi!

Then I get noticed. A woman wearing an apron beckons me to come upstairs. Unfortunately she doesn't speak English, luckily one of the other attendees does, her son as it turns out. I tell them I'm joining Xenia and Lefteris tonight, if that is considered appropriate of course.

"My mother says it's okay," the boy tells me. "She asks if you're Paul."

I nod. The woman grabs me firmly with both hands and kisses me on the cheeks. She then shows me the chapel and from what I understand, people just sit outside during the service. The chapel is seriously tiny. Behind the altar is a spot where the 'Pappas' will be standing tonight. The choir singers will be standing in the chapel, she tells me. The chapel is decorated beautifully, with frescoes, a copper candle table and icons behind glass are placed alongside the walls. Gold foil has been used everywhere as decoration. Behind the chapel is a small house. "My family lived here," the woman says, using her son as an interpreter, "tonight my great-aunt will be present, she's ninety-two years old."

A yard of poured concrete surrounds the entire chapel and the house, which has been limed white along the edges. Naturally the whole yard is surrounded by a low wall, which is also white. There are some rags hanging on the wall. It looks very colorful. And there are pots and feta cans filled with plants everywhere. Olive and fig trees grow as far as the eye can see. This place simply breathes history. She pulls me towards the path upward. There's a ruin of what once was a small house. "They have always lived in this 'Kalivi'. But it has no water and electricity, which explains why the new house was built. Since the passing of her sister a few years ago, my great-aunt has been living in the village."

"The chapel has been built here, because the holy Irini appeared on this exact spot once. My family has always done their very best to maintain it properly."

"It looks beautiful," I say. She then apologizes through her son. "There are a lot of people coming tonight and my mother still has to prepare a lot."

The terrace is a lovely place, especially under these olive trees. I look forward to sitting here tonight.
I have been studying Greek Orthodox worship and Name-days on the internet last night. And Lefteris was right, it is nothing like the church services held in Dutch Protestant and Roman Catholic churches that I know.
The Pappas sings the scriptures and will be assisted in this by choristers. There won't be a lot of preaching, but there will be room for the profession of faith and for praying as well.
I personally love Gregorian hymns and I hope that tonight might present me with something similar.

I arrive at exactly a quarter to seven at Xenia's and Lefteris' place. But Xenia is not ready yet, she still needs to water the plants and change her clothes. The service starts at seven o'clock but apparently I'm the only one who worries about being late. Lefteris is casually drinking a beer and offers me one too.

At half past seven we arrive at the chapel. There are cars parked everywhere, mostly askew. At the chapel, there is already an enormous crowd. Xenia takes me to a long table where people can place bread, wine and olive oil as a sacrifice. In the middle behind the table sits a very aged woman, flanked by old men. "This is Nina Paul, she is the hostess tonight as this is her property."

I whisper to Xenia: "Can I call her Nina?"

Xenia smiles: "Yes, that's her name."

Nina embraces Xenia warmly. She is very old, but it's clearly visible that she must have been an exceptionally beautiful woman. She has a somewhat mischievous, smiling face. I turn to greet Nina. I extend my hand out to her across the table with the bread, wine and oil. I try to bend a little, to show my respect for her. My hand is ignored completely. The little woman stands up, reaches to my head with both hands, grabs me and kisses me on both cheeks. She says something in Greek, and looks at me, giggling. Everyone laughs and Xenia translates; "She thinks you're a handsome man and she asks if you are rich and available." Nina's cheeks turn pink. I have her hands in mine and look at her: "Thank you Nina, shall we turn this into a wedding then?"

There is laughter as Xenia translates. I learn fast, as I wrote before. The table of old men at Aggelos' taught me that you can say anything here, as long as you're cheerful and happy.

Lefteris and I sit down on one of the walls with the rugs on top. This gives us a good view. The large copper table holding candles, which was still inside the chapel this morning, now stands just outside the entrance to the chapel. People are constantly lighting candles in front of it. The boy who interpreted for me this morning evidently got the task of removing the half-burned candles, so there is room for new ones. There is an icon at the entrance to the chapel which is being kissed by all visitors. A young man is walking around the place, installing audio equipment. He should be about thirty-five years old and is wearing pale blue linen trousers and a white linen shirt. He wears his long black hair in a ponytail, and deftly climbs into an olive tree to readjust the speaker hanging there.
"That's the Pappas" says Lefteris, pointing to him. I'm surprised.
Everyone is chattering, children are running through the crowd. We only see Xenia occasionally, when she

walks by while being immersed in a conversation with a few women. The clock in the teeny-tiny bell tower begins to ring and then it all starts.

The Pappas welcomes us through the speaker. He is standing in the chapel and is thus not visible to the public.

Suddenly everyone is standing up and begins to cross themselves, while muttering along with Pappas' voice sounding loudly through the microphone.

When his prayer has ended, the people sit down again and resume their conversations while Pappas begins singing his songs.

Despite the buzz of dozens of people talking, people coming and going and the playing of children, I can hear the chants of Pappas very well. His beautiful tenor voice sounds clear and flimsy and from time to time the choristers accompany him. I get carried away.

It is a remarkable gathering. The singing of verses seems endless and is interrupted only by prayer. When this happens, everyone stands up, people cross themselves multiple times, pray and sit back again while resuming conversations with their neighbor. Suddenly everything goes quiet, everyone is standing up. Lefteris briefly touches my hand to notify me. I can see the priest coming out of the chapel. He is now wearing a magnificent gold-embroidered robe on top of his dusty clothes. On his head he has some sort of miter. He has a censer in his right hand, the chain in his left hand. He walks past people and blesses them one by one.

And suddenly he stands in front of me. I realize too late, that everyone else cast their glances down in his presence. I look him straight in his brown eyes. He looks back at me, first decisively and boldly, then he softens his eyes and his mouth slowly forms an almost imperceptible smile. Without wanting it, without expecting it to happen, I can feel a big tear rolling off my cheek. Almost invisibly, he nods at me. There is a wave of emotion going through me.

When the priest is back inside and has resumed his hymns, I just sit there, petrified, staring into nothing. Xenia hops along, puts her hand on my head and says, "Nice eh, Paul!"

Then she hops away again. Lefteris sigh and looks for my hand. He saw my tear and felt my emotions.
And we sit like that for a while, Lefteris and I. Hand in hand. I am intensely happy.

My Ithaca

Dimi, while I was still in school, in grammar school to be precise, I was taught Ancient Greek.
It was something my mother was actually very good at. She helped me with my homework, quizzed me and had me read texts from the old school books that she still owned.
I can't exactly remember in which class I was when we read the Iliad and the Odyssey. I'll be honest with you though, I didn't read the original texts but the Dutch translations. Not because I was lazy, but rather because I did not want to miss anything. I thought it was a wonderful story and thoroughly enjoyed reading it.
Later, I read the books in Greek as well with a little help from my mother.
It was my first introduction to a story that tells the reader something other than it literally says. I learned that from my mother as well; the appearance of symbolism.

My mother used to ask me: "Who is Penelope?" And I replied, "The wife of Odysseus."

My mother then asked me; "And what does she symbolize?" And I remained silent.

That moment, my magnificent quest for the true meaning of the Odyssey began, together with her. Penelope symbolized happiness and security in earlier times. Did you know that Dimi? I thought, no, I knew for sure that my mother was my Penelope. And I still believe it.

According to my mother, the trip to Troy, the war and the devastation were a symbolical break with the 'old ways', the old structure and order in Odysseus' life. He severed it all, he destroyed Troy.

His return to Ithaca, a journey that never seemed to end because the gods were not favorable to him, opposed him even. Dimi, that retreat was Odysseus' struggle to deal with everything that seemed to have been dear to him until then: status, power, wealth, but also the comrades he lost during his journeys. You could say that Odysseus purged himself of all those old values in order to experience his return exposed and bare. The return to Ithaca, a return in itself.

When my mother taught and told me all those things, the luster of the story suddenly disappeared because of the person I was then.

But yesterday, while sitting in the kitchen with the letters I wrote to you Dimi, I suddenly started to remember.

Is that why you left me? Because you wanted to make the journey of Odysseus and I still lacked the courage?

Then you had much more insight than I did at an early stage already, and I really never knew you at all.

I wrote that I felt particularly victimized as a result of our breakup. And I wrote that from my heart. I never knew you thought of me as a rigid dick, unwilling to share even the slightest bit of all the material wealth I had accumulated over time. Powerless in my inability to love myself. Powerless in being who I truly wanted to be.

I always believed I lived a proper and righteous life. I have worked hard for everything. But I've never really asked myself whether I truly desired everything I owned.

While I'm telling you this Dimi, I realize it's you who became the victim and not the other way around.

How come you never told me? Why did you never include me in your dreams?

It doesn't matter how you look at it Dimi, you were home sooner than I was. It was your right to choose that road.
I get it now. And that's painful, for I am indeed a coward and a self-centered one at that. Everything was nice as long as it fit into my schedule. I speak using numbers, numbers are like words to me. But numbers are cold and numb. I get it now Dimi. The cup is empty.

My holiday is almost over. I decide to buy Liesbeth a gift, for the very first time in fifteen years. I pick a brooch, a pretty one. It cost me two hundred and fifty euro, which makes it a ridiculously expensive gift for one's secretary, but I truly want to do something nice for her just this once. In addition, she likes to wear brooches. She uses them to arrange the scarves draped around her shoulders. I've decided I'm going to do everything differently. I'm going to give more. Overcome my fears. I also want to spread joy, like the people on this island do. I want to give more meaning

to the actual human being that I am, instead of focusing solely on concepts such as status and wealth.
This holiday has been strange, unreal. I've done things I never did before. I flew a charter plane, spoke with all and sundry, sat at a table with old men whose language I do not speak. But that didn't throw up any barriers. I ate on the street, I cried and laughed. How long ago have I even done these things with so much passion? I kissed in public, kissed men and women. There are two things I need to do, apart from saying goodbye to all the people who made such a deep impression on me.

Firstly, I want to go up to that little church, considering I still have an unfinished conversation waiting there for me. And secondly I want to visit Stafilos. I understand that you liked going there Dimi, so I need to take a look at the place.

When I leave here, I will take a totally different image of Greeks with me as well as a newly found love for the sun, the heat that makes the people here so hot-blooded.

I surrendered to the chaos that Greeks create. And now I understand their resentment against authority, against tyranny. Not counting the parasitic types obviously.

Dimi, I belong to those parasites. I work at a financial institution that has been making money off ordinary people for years. It has certainly paid off for me and only now do I understand the gravity of the situation. I want to speak using words again, not numbers. Dimi, I'm going to do everything differently.

I spoke to a broker yesterday about selling the house. I don't need to make a profit out of it. I have enough. Thus the broker expects the house to be sold quickly. I will give the plants I bought for the balcony to the neighbor, since she brought me fresh tomatoes from her garden every single day during the recent weeks. The fact that I'm going to sell the house might feel like betrayal to you Dimi, but what would I do with it anyway? I might never come back here. Catherina has promised to look for a fitting charity that I could donate the proceeds to, in these difficult times an institution like that shouldn't be too hard to find though.

I buy a ticket for the ferry at the ticket office, not for the Cat though. I don't want to sit on a water bus, in rows behind each other. I don't want to get to Skiathos fast, rather calmly and peacefully. I want to be on the ferry to enjoy the organized chaos on the docks with all the people and the cars. 'Chaos' is actually a well-chosen Greek word.

Tonight is my last night. People are moving back to the village to eat and drink, to talk and to watch football together with people they do not know. I'm heading to the chapel. I have come to love this community.
From afar, I can see the Pappas sitting near the wall. My mother would consider the stairs as being symbolic.
I'm not the only one who is climbing the stairs, a lot of people go up every day, I saw them climb when I was at Aggelos' restaurant sitting at the old men's table. Now I'm the one working my old body up the steep stairs. Finally I reach the top. I burn a candle for Dimi and for my father and mother. I don't see any chairs, so when I feel I'm alone for a moment, I briefly fold my hands while standing. I explain to God that I was mad at him, but I finally came to understand that I was angry with myself. I also explain to God that I consider my journey to this island a victory, not a fiasco. I speak to God about the opacity of his intentions, and how it is sometimes

difficult for us people to recognize them. It's nice to ponder these subjects in silence. Every piece of the puzzle has finally found its correct destination. The cup is empty. Thank you for my lovely holiday.

I go outside and walk up to the priest. He touches my hand very lightly, while giving me an intrusive but friendly look. He gives me a small picture of the Virgin Mary with Jesus on her lap. "Thank you," I say, he crosses himself and blesses me.

I go to Janis' bar, the place I visited almost every day during the past three weeks. The bar is beautiful, Janis is fun and the waiters, who are all students from Thessaloniki, are artistic. The music Janis plays is always carefully chosen. My favorite spot on the terrace is the bench against the wall, from there I can see the whole harbour. I take a seat there again. Whenever I'm here, I can feel an immense peace flow through me. I drink three cocktails and kiss Janis on his cheeks, he firmly holds my shoulders. Then I wander off through the narrow streets to Perivoli, Yorgos' restaurant. I've eaten here three times, Yorgos is a good chef and the entourage is great.

Yorgos cries when I tell him goodbye. He doesn't have much time as the restaurant is fully booked, so I thank him for everything he has done for Dimi. Yorgos stays behind all alone, I have to admit that I feel sorry for him.

Since I've learned that language doesn't have to be a barrier in establishing contacts, I sit down on a curb next to an old man. We talk using gestures and nods mostly.

Farewell old man, I'm going to miss you all.

It's around half past twelve and I still want to go to Stafilos, the beach Dimi liked to visit.

I drive my scooter as slow as possible. I look around me quietly, the wind feels hot on my face. I didn't button up my shirt. I'm wearing shorts and slippers which I bought in the store with Italian menswear. I need to drive down a little path once I'm near Stafilos. I see hotels and restaurants on either side of the winding road, I hear people talking, laughing on the terraces. I park the scooter at the end of the road. To get to the beach I have to go down some stairs. It's quite dark between the trees, even though there's a full moon overhead. I nearly trip once but manage to regain my balance. After a gentle curve I can see the beach appearing below me. I feel the need to stop and pause for a second. The view in front of me is more beautiful than the most beautiful painting. The moon illuminates the water, the sand and the cliffs in thousands of shades, acting as a multiplier. Gray, green, dark blue, yellow-green, blue-green, gray blue... I'm utterly speechless.

I walk down slowly. I take off my slippers once I'm on the beach and continue walking barefoot on the cool sand, in the direction of the rippling water caressing the sand.

I sit down and look out over the sea. It is so wonderfully beautiful that I'm unable to move for a long time. I am all alone on this beach and the only thing I can hear is the splashing water and a distant buzz coming from a terrace. I look at the perfectly round moon and thousands of stars above the silky-looking sea. Stafilos was the son of Ariadne and Dionysus according to Greek mythology. Dionysus was the god of just about everything, but above all he was the god of connection. If his son inherited even the slightest hint of this trait, then this might the place where Dimi and I can be connected to each other again.

So here I am. A small wave tickles my toes.

I suddenly realize that I haven't even swum in the beautiful clear waters surrounding the island, for the past three weeks.

But I have no swimsuit with me I'm afraid.

It is almost reason enough to stay put. "If you go swimming in your underwear, it'll be wet when you go back on the scooter, Paul. You'll catch a cold!"

I decide not to listen to the voice and take off my clothes instead, all of them, and slowly walk into the sea, naked. Once the water has reached my thighs, I immerse myself completely. The water feels like cool silk. My skin tingles. I swim. While I move my hands, slowly, as slowly as possible, I can feel it caressing my skin.

My fingers play with the water, and in the moonlight I can see my white feet slowly moving under the water. I turn around and lie on my back. Stretch myself out completely, arms wide. I'm drifting while looking at the moon and stars above me. I am drifting, being carried…

The Homecoming

It's the morning of my departure. I did not sleep well last night. I'm afraid that the charter and related hassle might disenchant me from my fairytale.
Lefteris is waiting for me at the shop where I rented the scooter, as agreed. We will all share a last lunch together, after which they'll take me to the port. I managed to bring my suitcase on the scooter, between my legs.
Lefteris smiles when he sees me coming; "You look like a Greek" as he points to the suitcase.
We get in the car, and chat in the same amiable way we have been getting used to over the past three weeks. I have a good relationship with Lefteris. He is a quietly profound and wise man. I like him and wonder what will happen to our early developed contact once I'm back in the Netherlands.
Xenia has already hinted she would like to visit me in the Netherlands. "We will be in Frankfurt again from

January and Lefteris won't bat an eyelid at driving such a short distance."

When we arrive at their house, Xenia has already set the table. She made pita bread, a tasty salad and souvlaki. I eat and drink beer. We talk, or rather, Xenia talks. I adore her, she is so wonderfully dominant and yet so devoted to me and Lefteris.
"I like the fact that you visited, Paul. It feels like, somehow, I have my little brother back in my life because of you."
"You have experienced Greeks for three whole weeks now, don't let them scare you away" Lefteris says, "most of them are good, hardworking people. They despise tyranny. I have a CD for you with music that originated during the general regime, in the seventies of the last century. They call it Greek Fado. But they're nonetheless beautiful poems, which have been converted to music. All those texts breathe the desire for freedom. To me, this music represents the essence of the Greeks. It was during this specific period, that many Greeks left abroad. Like Xenia and me. To us this period of the general regime is a black page in our history. Greeks are a freedom-loving people, but that also has its downsides." Lefteris shifts in his

chair. He has some issues with his back but, apart from restlessly shifting on a chair, it's hardly noticeable.

"The downside Paul, is that we Greeks do not like to interfere in the affairs of others. We simply wish for everyone to enjoy freedom in life. There is no need for control. However, when you combine this with the generally well known Mediterranean laissez-faire mentality, then the crisis that hit us is not so surprising. The result is that the distrust in our government has grown even bigger than before. I am Greek and I always will be. I love this country, but after spending thirty years Germany I can unerringly put the finger on the sore spot. You too I think Paul, as a Dutchman and a banker at that."

He smiles, but in his eyes I see a hint of annoyance too.

"It bothers me that I have so much love for this country, and at the same time can see so clearly why it all went wrong."

I reassure Lefteris. All the Greeks I've met, I've come to love. The island is beautiful and the climate is wonderful. To cheer up Xenia and Lefteris I tell them, that Dimi once told me that Greece has a distinctive scent.

"That's right," I tell them "and that scent will always stay with me."

Sharp-wittedly, Xenia remarks that I sound as if I will never come back. For the second time in my life, I leave my true intentions about coming back to Skopelos in the middle.

I do not think I will come back. Why would I do that? But I'm not telling them.

Lefteris and Xenia take me to the docks. We say goodbye to each other. I ask them not to wait until the ferry departs. I still have not been able to release all my fears and am afraid that I'm going to cry when they wave at me from the wharf.

There I am, a part of a clump of people again, who will all be storming the ferry shortly when the signal is given, between cars and trucks, with suitcases and packages, shouting at each other, laughing and crying. I look forward to that moment.

I see the ferry turning in the bay of the harbour. A little while longer and it'll moor. Then my adventure will almost be over.

While I'm out there, images of the past three weeks bubble up again. Lost in own my thoughts I hear the voice of the first mate through the microphone, then the rattling of chains, the cars, the people who greet their loved ones. But we're still waiting. It's not our turn yet.

Slowly it dawns on me, that someone is constantly shouting my name.

I turn around and there, at the entrance of the port, I see Xenia. She is waving at me with one hand, her other hand is holding up a package. That's the food she wrapped up for me and that I forgot to bring along.

I look at the ferry, they are still unloading. There is yet some time left to quickly walk to Xenia to pick up the package.

I walk towards her, it's only twenty meters, but now I'm back facing the village. And in those few steps to Xenia I see Janis' terrace, where I was looking at the harbor while listening to his beautiful music. More to the right I see Aggelos' restaurant, where I sat on a daily basis at the old men's table where I was invited while the blame, my blame, weighed so heavily upon me. And above the restaurant I see the white chapel. The cross on the dome forms a bright contrast against the clear blue sky. I think of the Pappas and his bright eyes with which he passed on the love of God to his listeners. Right in front of me I see the bakery where I bought bread every day, and behind it, a bit to the right, I should be able to see the balcony of my house. My home...

"You forgot your food." I'm in front of Xenia and grab the plastic bag from her hands. In my other hand I have my ticket ready for inspection by port officials. I look at the little piece of paper in my hand and then look at Xenia, beautiful Xenia, and I ask; "Xenia, do you, by any chance, have a good reason to go to Skiathos today?"
Startled, she looks at me, for a brief moment she doesn't understand but then her dark eyes begin to sparkle. She wraps her arms tightly around my waist and hides her face in my chest. She is crying. She is so small that I don't even feel her hair against my chin.
She grabs my hands.
"Paul," she says, beaming through her tears, "what would you say if we go and drink a whole bottle of Retsina at Janis' place." Tears run down both her cheeks.

She takes my hand and walks with me to the exit of the ferry wharf. Lefteris is standing there with the car door already open.

"We will ask him to pick us up later, ok?"

So there I am, walking and holding hands with a woman. She knows I was her brother's lover, yet she loves me. She is my friend, and I hold her hand. We laugh and skip like adolescents, when I hear the noise of a departing ferry behind me.

And now it has been accomplished, dear readers, in fact it could not have ended any other way. Let's face it. This was indeed the way everything should have turned out! You already knew it. But silly me, I knew nothing, I understood nothing. I thought the cup was empty, but there were still a few drops left.

The need for peace within me has always been unmistakably present, and now I have found it. And so it is finished, it could not end otherwise.

I lay in bed. The night is dark and feels thick somehow. I can almost grasp the darkness. But in my head, my voice sounds like I'm in a big empty space, my voice echoes.

My name is Paul van den Berg, I am sixty years old and gay. Not that I really care, I'm just stating a fact... I feel warm and proud.

Mom, today I came home. My Odyssey is over. It feels like liberation, mom. Is this the Kingdom of God you always told me about?

The story of Els Boot

When I was just a child, I had a little table in my bedroom that was painted orange and blue. It had a drawer in the middle. In that drawer, I stashed my notebooks and a pair of my dad's old glasses. I considered a pair of glasses as something essential for writing, and since I wrote stories and poems in those notebooks.

Those glasses remain, as well as the stories. When I was seven years old though, I got my own glasses and since then I have been become more and more near-sighted, because eye sight simply deteriorates throughout the years. The stories, well even those remained. At one point, I got involved into politics. Even became a mayor. But that specific combination, writing and politics, hasn't always been understood. Nevertheless, it actually makes sense. For politics require imagination and a genuine love for people and their motives. Perhaps many politicians have forgotten this, which is very unfortunate. Because if there's anything we need in this world, it is definitely politicians with a keen imagination. All those years filled with endless meetings and busy schedules kept pulling at 'the pen'. In those lost hours, I created novels in my mind, wrote timelines and sometimes I even constructed a few pages. But it never progressed beyond that. All my ideas disappeared in a drawer. Just like the one I had as a child. I diverted my imagination into speeches instead, which I always wrote myself.

But lately, I experienced the luxury of having more time on my hands. So I finally started to concentrate more on writing. It makes me happy. Writing is a passion of mine as well as a magical process.

From the author

The story about this quest by Paul van den Berg sprouted after my friend Dimitris died of a heart attack. In the years that I've known him, he often told me about this friend that he had in the Netherlands. The last time I spoke Dimitris he said he planned to visit him again, after forty years. Unfortunately he never got the chance to do this. A few months later Dimitris died.

I forgot the name of his Dutch friend and because of this, could not search for him. Gradually the idea for this story was created. It is actually not a novel but more of a narrative or a trip report in a metaphorical sense. I deliberately chose to tell the story through the eyes of Dimitris' friend. This way, the death of Dimitris feels not without significance. The comparison with Homer's Odyssey is therefore logical.

Review

If you enjoyed reading this story, I would appreciate it very much if you could take the time to write a review on Amazon.com

You can contact me through my website
www.elsboot.com

Twitter @authorelsboot
Facebook authorElsBoot

Thanks

I would like to thank everybody who helped me with writing this story.
I would like to thank Natasja Jankowy for translating. She is a young start-up and a courageous single mother. You can always contact her for translations through LinkedIn.